# *Prevailing* PRAYER

*Unleash the Royal Prayer Warrior Within*

ROSETTA BERNASKO

Copyright © 2017 Rosetta Bernasko.

This book or parts thereof may not be reproduced in any form, stored in a retrieval system or transmitted in any form by any means – electronic, mechanical, photocopy, recording or otherwise – without prior written permission of the publisher, except as provided by United States of America copyright law.

ISBN: 978-0-9992152-0-3 Paperback
ISBN: 978-0-9992152-1-0 Ebook

Unless otherwise noted, all Scripture quotations are from King James Version of the Bible.

Scripture quotations marked NIV are from the Holy Bible, New International Version.

Copyright © 1973, 1978, 1984, International Bible Society. Used by permission

Scripture quotations marked AMPC are from the Holy Bible, Amplified Bible, Classic Edition

Copyright © 1954, 1958, 1964, 1965, 1987, The Lockman Foundation. Used by permission

Scripture quotations marked ERV are from the Holy Bible, Easy to Read Version
Copyright © 1978, 1987, 2012 Bible League International. Used by permission

Scripture quotations marked NLT are from the Holy Bible, New Living Translation Version

Copyright © 1996, 2004, 2007 Tyndale House Foundation. Used by permission

Scripture quotations marked GNT are from the Holy Bible, Good News Translation 2nd Edition

Copyright © 1992 American Bible Society. Used by permission

All quotes by great men of prayer taken from www.azquotes.com

Cover Design by Janet Dado and Jose Pepito Jr
Book Layout by Jose Pepito Jr

# CONTENTS

Foreword ............................................................................. v

Acknowledgements .......................................................... vii

Dedications ........................................................................ ix

Introduction ....................................................................... xi

    First Things First ..................................................... xxiii

Chapter 1    Pitiful to Powerful ............................................ 1

Chapter 2    Platform for Prevailing Prayer ...................... 13

Chapter 3    The Perils of Prayerlessness .......................... 31

Chapter 4    God's Purpose for Creating Man ................. 43

Chapter 5    Kingdom Keys for Prevailing Prayer ........... 58

Chapter 6    Work the Word & Will His Will into Your World ... 74

Chapter 7    Christ In Me, The Hope of Glory ............... 101

Chapter 8    Fired Up for the Faith Fight ....................... 116

Chapter 9    Enter the Dragon, Your Adversary ............. 140

Chapter 10    The Practice of Prevailing Prayer ............... 163

Prologue ......................................................................... 185

# FOREWORD
## by Pastor Kwaku Marfo

Prayer is an important part of our Christian lives. It gives the believer the opportunity to commune with God in many ways. The things we bring before God in prayer are often an expression of the issues on our hearts and what we are fervent about.

Many Christians have adopted a superficial attitude towards prayer and trivialized it. We go to God by reciting things in a routine and inattentive manner. When that happens, prayer becomes unproductive and inconsequential. The first few verses of Luke 11, make it clear that, prayer involves a pattern that needs to be taught. After spending a lot of time with Jesus, one of His disciples came to Him and said, *"Lord, teach us to pray, as John also taught his disciples"* (Luke 11:1b). This implies that prior to Jesus's establishment of a pattern of prayer for His disciples, John the Baptist had also taught his disciples the way to pray. It is interesting that only one out of the twelve disciples asked Jesus to teach them to pray. The fact is, sometimes the church or Christians seem to be in a similar situation today regarding prayer. Many Christians are failing to earnestly look for how they ought to pray. But there is a need for clear direction about this crucial tenet of our faith.

In this book, "Prevailing Prayer: Unleashing the Royal Prayer Warrior Within", Rosetta Bernasko provides comprehensive answers to the most frequently-asked questions about prayer. The ten chapters of this book will ignite in the reader an earnest passion to pray and see positive results in their lives. I have no doubts that readers will be challenged to deepen their communion with God through prayer.

Rosetta has spent a copious amount of her time over the years, in the Word of God and prayer, and has put together this book to help readers gain deeper insights into attaining a productive prayer life. All her Word-based ideas in this book are at the very core of her personal passion for prayer.

"Prevailing Prayer: Unleashing the Royal Prayer Warrior Within" is must read book for all Christians, and has come at an auspicious time in the history of the Church. I recommend the book as an effective workshop model on prayer for all churches. I trust that every page of this book will inspire readers to pray more and experience a major move of God in their lives.

Pastor Kwaku Marfo,
Exaltation Temple, International
Central Gospel Church (ICGC)
Delaware, USA

# ACKNOWLEDGEMENTS

To My One Faithful Friend, the Lord Jesus Christ Himself:

Thank you for your great sacrifice on the Cross, for never giving up on me and putting up with all the complexities of me. Thank you, lover of my soul, for walking with me and shaping me through every mountain and valley and for entrusting me with this book to share with your people. Lord, Here's to many more days of our Pilgrim's Progress journey!

To my Dearly Loved, Always Dependable and Highly Esteemed Husband Stanley:

Thank you for supporting me in this venture, and for being such a great Husband, Father and Provider. None of this would have been possible without you by my side.

To the lovely angels God gave me, Victoria and Valencia. Mommy loves you so much!

To the World's Best Parents, Ted and Araba Bernasko:

Dad and Mom, thank you from the bottom of my heart for your unconditional and consistent support. I love you more than words can say!

To Abby Farmer:

Thank you for your marvelous contributions to the editing of this book. I am so grateful to the Lord for connecting me with you.

To my Pastors, Bishop Matthew C. Haskell and Pastor Monica Haskell:

Thank you for modeling the Word of God, for faith and fire and the five-fold gifts that flow through our church. Your sound Words have helped Stan and I tremendously. Thank you!

# DEDICATIONS

This book is dedicated to my Esteemed Prayer Leader, Pastor Owusu-Achim:

Thank you for being my prayer covering. Connecting with you and the Peace and Wisdom Prayer Conference has catapulted me, my prayer life and ministry into new dimensions for which I praise God and thank you. Thank you for believing in me. God bless you and Mama Christabel.

# INTRODUCTION

> ²*Lord, I have heard of your fame; I stand in awe of your deeds, Lord. Repeat them in our day, in our time make them known; in wrath remember mercy. (Habakkuk 3:2, NIV)*

Dear Fellow Believer,

Thank you for picking up this book. I have been praying specifically for you and it's no coincidence that our paths are crossing. You are already on God's mind and He will continue to go to extra-ordinary lengths to provide everything you need that pertains to life and godliness (Phil. 4:19) to live and thrive in this life because you are that important to Him.

I suspect that you are checking out this book for at least one of the following reasons:

- ❖ You are a seeker trying to gain more knowledge on the Christian faith and prayer specifically.
- ❖ You are a nominal or new Christian looking to learn about prayer.
- ❖ You are an active Christian, doing all the right things on the outside, but on the inside, you are yearning for a deeper relationship with God.
- ❖ You know that your existing prayer life needs to be infused with new knowledge and deeper insight.

Or you are experiencing one of these life circumstances:

- ❖ You are tired of a life that seems out of control.
- ❖ Your life seems to be marked with defeat, degradation, delay, disappointments, and disillusion.
- ❖ Your prayers don't seem to make much of a difference when you do pray, so you view prayer as a hit or miss proposition that leaves you preferring to do other things instead.

Whatever your back story, even if you don't quite fit into any of the above, welcome, all the same. You are in the right place and this book is for you. If you are not yet born again, please check out the section First Things First at the very end of this chapter first because it is the critical first step in your journey toward a more victorious prayer and overall Christian life.

Your quest to change your current spiritual state has brought you here. You want to gain deeper insights into attaining a productive prayer life. Well, God loves you so much and cares for your specific needs that He has orchestrated things just so He can have you where you need to be. You know fully well that no effective prayer life exists outside of a vibrant engaged relationship with God in His entirety: Father, Son, and Holy Spirit—yes, the Holy Spirit too! No branch of a fruit tree can produce abundant, healthy fruit without drawing nutrients from the tree (John 15:4). This is because we simply can't expect to just ask God for things without having any other communication with Him or knowledge of Him. He loves us and wants us to actively love Him back.

<u>Prevailing Prayer: Unleash The Royal Prayer Warrior Within</u> is for anyone who wants to touch God and see His mighty hands move in their circumstances as they pray. This book is designed to help you acquire the fundamental knowledge, skills, and abilities that are necessary to have a productive, powerful, results-oriented prayer life.

Prayer can be hard work, especially in the beginning stages. In the same way that gold and diamonds are rarely found on the surface, you have to dig deep to find the rewards of a rich prayer life. The true treasures of prayer rarely come to anyone who is cavalier about finding and enjoying the benefits of prayer. There must be a deliberate, focused, and persistent approach to prayer – traits that don't come naturally to me because of my temperament! I actually consider it an astounding irony that God has birthed this ministry through me and made me a Christian Mindset Coach and Prayer Consultant to help others live in victory through an overall victorious Christian lifestyle that I am calling "Pray, Slay, and Reign". The very fact this book (the first of a trilogy) is in your hands is evidence of God doing the impossible through me. I am a shining and eternally grateful example of the truism that **God doesn't call the qualified, He qualifies the called.**

Therefore, don't despair if you think you are in any way inadequate to truly be everything God in His perfect Will called you and is requiring you to be. The absence of the innate abilities that promote a powerful prayer life isn't in its own right a problem for God because He can dramatically change anything, and especially when it comes to molding us into His image so we can accomplish His expectations, He is more than able to work with us if we are willing to work with Him, no matter how quickly or long it takes. He calls those things that are not there into existence or manifestation.

Consider the powerful encounters that occurred between Jesus and individuals who put their faith in Him! The Samaritan woman at the well was transformed for a social outcast to an evangelist (John 4). He can literally resurrect dead things! Remember Jesus called Lazarus from the grave (John 12)?

We know that the call to climb the mountain of prayer isn't insurmountable or an impossible mission because we know that God says if we draw near to Him, He will draw near to us (James 4:8). When we commit to seeking after God, He is with us in each step of the struggle! We aren't stranded and alone! He is able to reach down His hand and lift us with His strength when we need Him. He will reward us for our efforts, if we will continue to press in. Therefore, if you commit to applying these timeless truths and secrets to your life, you will surely see your spiritual life increase in all kinds of good things. Instead of focusing on the rocky trail ahead of us, prayer helps us to look up and see the beauty of the surroundings instead of worrying about the rocky trail itself.

This book emphasizes educating you first in the Word and then coaching you into effectively practicing what has been taught through practical application. Each chapter provides plenty doses of scripture, carefully explained and then how-to tips and related prayer points. Additionally, there is an accompanying Prevailing Prayer Journal/Workbook and training material on our website, www.prayslayandreign.com. This combination catapults engaged readers away from simply participating in passive reading exercises which only produce head knowledge and into the realm of a practical results-oriented prayer life! This becomes the active pursuit of an intimate, growing, and productive relationship with the Lord.

## A LITTLE ABOUT MY JOURNEY

I consider myself a very ordinary Christian. I wasn't a sinner of notorious reputation with a dramatic conversion story like the Apostle Paul (Acts 9). I was born again just before becoming a teenager. I loved the Lord and learning about Him even in my early Christian years. I was fortunate to be enrolled at a great boarding school a few years before an awesome revival broke out and so in addition to great educational and spiritual teaching, I had the luxury of friends who were also hungry for God. Those were some heady times, being a front-row witness to some pretty incredible acts of God! Many of us got filled with the Holy Spirit with the evidence of speaking in tongues, and some of my schoolmates were soon flowing in spiritual gifts and great anointing and power. Our corporate weekly Bible Fellowship services were just incredible with excellent praise and worship, moves of the Holy Spirit, and demonstrations of the power of God.

Outside of services, my friends and I spent many hours discussing the Bible, praying with and encouraging each other. We had an hour of mandatory siesta with no talking allowed and during that time, I would typically listen to Christian music, spend lots of time engaging with the Lord by reading and studying the Word. Other times I would listen to sermons on a forbidden Walkman (yes it was

*Introduction*

a very strict school) by great preachers and teachers and pray quietly by myself. To this day, I love Christian music and spent many hours immersing my spirit man in solid Word-based Christian music. I was a fairly decent Believer and tried to always do the right thing and live for God. I expected nothing but a happy easy-going life as a reward for my service. What could possibly go wrong? My Heavenly Father was there for me to protect me and guide me and I was implicitly sure and confident in this knowledge, especially since I had seen Him do so many amazing things at a very early age.

It wasn't until a few years after this amazing boarding school environment that as a young adult I realized that as much as I loved God, by myself and without the tight routine of boarding school life, I had great difficulty prioritizing prayer into my schedule. Truth be told, when it came to time carved out for prayer, more often than not, my mind wandered away every time I tried to pray! I would fall asleep as soon as I started to pray and it didn't matter what time of day it was. Nevertheless, I had some degree of success and or normalcy in the earlier years of my life and so in my naivety, I didn't perceive the real need to press into a lifestyle of prayer especially since I wasn't aware of anything pressingly persistent that needed fixing.

To compensate, I spent most of my free time listening to and singing Christian music, and in more Bible study. All of these things are good but not a substitute for prayer. I talked to the Lord disjointedly, but frequently as I went through my day, and sometimes used the lyrics of my songs as a way to pray. It was the only thing I knew to do to sustain myself spiritually and remain connected to God. I understood the value of prayer—if I really felt there was some extra need, I would pray the best I could and then tell a few other "prayer warriors" and friends to pray for me as well. I know many people who do this too: pass the buck on to others to do the heavy lifting of prayer for us, while we cross our fingers and cross ourselves, hoping our Hail Mary pass will work for the best. That strategy gave me some measure of success. I usually felt a good connection with God and continued to grow in some knowledge and grace of God.

Occasionally, I would go through seasons where the door of communication with God would suddenly and inexplicably swing shut. During those times, God seemed very far away and my usual routine of connecting with Him would become very cold. I would experience weakness and dryness but eventually, things would swing back and I would get back on track with the Lord. And so, I kept lurching along but now with the benefit of hindsight, I see that slowly I was becoming less powerful and discerning spiritually. In the meantime, I graduated from college, worked in corporate America, met my then barely-Christian husband and got married after three years of dating. A few years in, by my early thirties, my life had steadily become such a series of mishaps and bad luck and seemingly unending difficulties I knew I needed to hit the reset button and re-learn some things as well as acquire some new strategies if I was going to be successful in my faith walk.

    I have been blessed to have experienced some great personal miracles in my life. There have been times when God came to my rescue in an amazingly dramatic fashion and it was so clear He was there for me! God has answered my prayers when I was seemingly down to the wire in the worst possible situations. I have been humbled and truly come to appreciate His compassion and mercies toward me. I have never questioned our Father's love for me, or the reality of His existence. At the same time, in between those spectacular shows of His power, I experienced deep, on-going and intractable problems that just seemed to have no end in sight. Those times of being in a "valley" were very lonely and difficult. I felt powerless to overcome these problems and agonized long and hard about my situation. During those times, I was praying the best I could, but little of the relief I was desperate for seemed to come my way. The measure of relief I got was temporary or more like a stop-gap measure, while the underlying issues continued. Like a treatment for the symptoms without a cure for the disease but only worse because even the symptoms didn't seem to truly ease up and would flare back up again and again. Looking back now, I see that some of the things I did to solve these problems were really like re-arranging chairs on the Titanic's deck with the iceberg looming straight ahead on the horizon. This happened because I wasn't aligned with the Holy Spirit, which we will talk more about, or praying effectively. In order to really confront the deeper issues, I had to delve deep into prayer and open my heart to hear the things God wanted to show me and then follow through with obedience to His wisdom.

This, my friends, is how I became obsessed with prayer, specifically prayer that actually brings results. At the root of my obsession with uncovering the secrets for powerful and productive prayer lies one key verse Mark 9:23: "If thou canst believe, all things are possible to him that believeth." Because I knew that no matter how difficult my life seemed to be, my God was still bigger than my problems, that He was still the same, yesterday, today, and forever and He hadn't abandoned me! I just needed to see the things I believed and held so deeply in my heart about Him and my Christian faith as true materialize in my life. I felt like Habakkuk, who said to God (paraphrased): "Lord, we have heard of your fame, we have heard of your deeds, the amazing things our fathers told us you accomplished in times past. How about a repeat, Lord? We sure could use a fresh impartation and experience" (Habakkuk: 3:2).

How I wanted and needed a vibrant new connection with God! I wanted to implicitly trust God again with that child-like faith and walk in His power that would allow me to function spiritually at another dimension where all things are indeed possible. A dimension where I was intimately connected to Him and wasn't just wasting my time, praying and getting nothing for my time and energy. If all my spiritual activities were no more than an exercise in futility or a crapshoot, then I would be content to call it quits and say it was all make-believe. And let's be honest, who hasn't ever felt like giving up or worse still, actually gave up praying because it didn't seem to matter? But I had seen too much, knew too much, and had personally experienced too much about God to ever completely write Him off. I gave up praying quite a few times but always came back to the glaring truth that the missing piece was more in my hand to uncover than in His inability or unwillingness to deliver.

Thus began the intense quest for answers. Answers on what really works in prayer. Answers that have taken several years and multiplied tens of thousands of hours of distilling through sermons and books by some of the very greatest prayer giants subject matter experts in the area of prayer and spiritual warfare. My personal method includes careful study of the Word and weighing what I am being exposed to by discernment, prayer and lots of trial and error. The ones that passed muster by producing more consistent results were then absorbed, practiced even more and retained as vital foundational principles to be shared with the body of Christ. Nothing presented here is text book theory; it all comes real life lessons from the school of hard knocks and even more practice.

To be honest, prevailing prayer is a deep, multi-faceted gem, which no one person can ever claim to know every single thing about. We all know only in part and prayer in particular is a highly complex jigsaw puzzle that different people have different pieces of the puzzle to. Nevertheless, the Lord has graced me by uncovering many open secrets that have allowed me to say I have truly seen the God of Elijah at work in our modern everyday circumstances. I can confidently say that the little I do know really does work, and not just for me.

And this is where you come in, dear Friend. At some point in our faith, we have to "set aside childish ways" (1 Cor. 3:11) and the rudimentary aspects of the Christian faith (Heb. 6:1-2) and go from drinking milk to chewing tough meat (Heb. 5:12-14). We have to grow-up if we really want to experience the God of the Bible, not the watered-down modern-day version who seems barely able to keep up with the Original! He hasn't changed. *We* have. And to re-discover Him and know Him in the power of His might, we have to do the changing, not Him. We have to mature in our faith and realize that our identities are founded in who we are in Christ! Think about the difference between a hiker who goes on day hikes on weekends and a serious outdoorsperson who is training for a thru-hike of the Appalachian Trail! The second person is goal oriented and driven. In order to unleash the Royal Prayer Warrior within, you must want to see your Christian life change and be willing to put in the work needed to get the results you desire to see through prevailing prayer. These are the distinct steps that if you carefully go through will get you to a prevailing prayer life.

They are:

- Acquiring the Principles of Prevailing Prayer
- Executing and Acquiring the Practice of Prevailing Prayer
- Experiencing and Enjoying the Proof of Prevailing Prayer

## ACQUIRING THE PRINCIPLES OF PREVAILING PRAYER

We first uncover the fundamental biblical principles that must be understood in order to have the needed foundational understanding for prevailing prayer. Please be very intentional about assimilating these timeless fundamental truths about prayer, how God operates, who Jesus is and where we fit in His plan. You will experience a greater occurrence of answered prayers if you truly understand the big picture as well as the verses that support what you believe and are declaring in your prayer life. Therefore, ruminate over the verses provided. Ask for revelation. Question God if you need to, but ultimately, you must adopt His words your own. It is the truth you know that will make you free.

## EXECUTING AND ACQUIRING THE PRACTICE OF PREVAILING PRAYER

I want this book to actually transform your life but this can only happen if you next put into practice or execute on what you first took the time to spiritually assimilate while acquiring the principles of prevailing prayer. In order to facilitate the execution of prayer I have provided at the end of each chapter two sections called Thoughts and Tips and Prayer Points. They serve as an introduction to the more expanded Prevailing Prayer Workbook/Journal which accompanies this book. It is highly recommended that you get this workbook/journal.

In the Tips and Thoughts part I guide you to do some soul searching on the info covered and help you foster the right mindset and strategies by which the manifestation of your prayers can be set into motion. The aim of this section is to empower you to work through the process of thinking through the principles learned and formulating the concrete steps needed to take to ensuring a prevailing prayer lifestyle. It's easy to get excited about what we learn and have the best of intentions to put it to good use but as we well know, the road to hell is paved with lots of good intentions. The Tips and Thoughts section takes you beyond good intentions and into the realm of actualization by forcing you to think through and implement strategies to help you stick with praying effectively.

Obviously, when it's all said and done, actual praying must take place. "Well, duh", you might be thinking, dear Friend! I have to respectfully draw to your attention that it's very easy to talk, read and think about praying and everything else and still never actually get around to *doing* it. It takes willful determination to actually talk to God Himself as opposed to talking about Him, daydreaming about when you get your answered prayers or whatever else. Trust me, the struggle is real! Practice having bona fide conversations with Him. Make a commitment to yourself and to the Lord to make time for Him.

If we are going to be skilled warriors, we need lots of practice using our weapons of warfare so we know how to use them efficiently. Getting into our place of intimacy with God must be repeated as frequently as possible to develop the habit or practice of prayer. The provided prayer points (as well as your personal prayers which I urge you to capture in the Prevailing Prayer Workbook/Journal) are to be prayed meditatively, preferably out loud and repeatedly until you feel a release to move on. It doesn't have to be the exact words in the provided prayer points, but it is important you get the general idea at stake in each prayer point. There is no magic formula, but do ask the Holy Spirit to help you to pray in accordance with what He knows you need. He will often use a prayer point as a base to bring something else to the forefront of your mind to be tackled in prayer. Follow His leading. Then do it again and again and again. Don't stop praying.

## THE PROOF OF PREVAILING PRAYER

In the third stage, you will see greater proof or evidence of your work done in the first two stages. As you grow in the knowledge presented here, and apply them in your prayer regimen, you will find yourself walking softly under the guidance of the Lord, but carrying a big sword. Your spiritual connection to God will make you even more humble, and your sin footprint will decrease but your spiritual power will grow. You will have a bigger spiritual sword that fights back the enemy, that is able to enforce heaven's will on earth and produce many desirable results in our lives.

May the good Lord enable you to not just be a spectator, but a true partaker of these glorious exploits, a true Royal Prayer Warrior.

## KEY POINTERS TO KEEP IN MIND
### Recognize and Capture Rationalizations and Distractions

There is a reason 2 Corinthians 10:5 (NIV) says: "We demolish arguments and every pretension that sets itself up against the knowledge of God, and we take captive every thought to make it obedient to Christ." As you read this book, maybe even now, you will very likely be mentally confronted with all kinds of reasons to give up. You'll find yourself being distracted and sidetracked. You may find your interest waning and arguments will crop up, trying to derail you and keep you from truly engaging with the topics. This is normal! The enemy wants to distract us. Satan comes to steal, kill, and destroy (John 10:10), especially when it comes to undermining your Spiritual walk! If we are going to be successful in connecting with and knowing God, we must learn to silence the voice of rationale (the opposite of faith) that will often cause us to shrink back from God. It also helps to rehearse what you have already read to help reinforce what you are learning and counter-act the enemy's moves.

In Hebrews 11:6 (KJV) the Bible says: "But without faith it is impossible to please him: for he that cometh to God must believe that He is, and that he is a rewarder of them that diligently seek him."

If you focus on the last part of the verse, you will realize that your ability to overcome is assured if you will stay the course. You will be rewarded for diligently seeking God.

It is your job to carefully and frequently scrutinize your thoughts, feelings and the circumstances you find yourself in, and deal harshly with (demolish) anything that is counter-productive. Every one of those arguments must be counter-acted, or made captive, with scriptures from the Word of God, which is your weapon. Be on the lookout for distractions, which will suddenly abound, in the beginning, and especially as you start to see results. All these ploys meant to fight the acquisition of greater knowledge of God and subsequently, getting more answered prayers. There is a reason Hebrews 11:6 uses the word "diligently" to describe the process of seeking because you must be very **intentional** in the pursuit of God.

## Arriving at our Desired Destination

In order for your transformation into a Royal Prayer Warrior to take place, you must adopt supportive new habits or lifestyle choices because we know that success rarely ever just happens in a vacuum. Here are a few tips to get you to your desired destination of answered prayers more frequently and faster.

- ❖ Treat your prayer times like you would an important date, for example.
- ❖ Consider fasting on a more regular schedule.
- ❖ Find some system of accountability, perhaps an online or in-person community of like-minded people pursuing the same goals you are.
- ❖ Journal your prayer journey and be prepared to take notes as the Holy Spirit will surely speak to you or impress something upon your heart. You will also want to capture things that cross your mind but need time to ponder over and address at a later time. Oftentimes, what is being impressed upon us is something that seems small or inconsequential yet if studied, meditated on and prayed over, God will bring additional illumination and use it to bring us victory. Be sure to not just catalogue your prayers, but to also capture God's responses to them over time. You will be able to see your own maturity evolve over time and witness God's answers to prayer as you make notations of His answers! Each prayer and answer to builds up your faith for even more.

Like David, you will be able to say, "I killed, the bear, I killed the lion, I will kill Goliath too!" (1 Samuel 17:36).

May this book truly empower you, dear Reader, and give you grace to accomplish many great things that you may never have counted yourself capable of achieving in the mighty name of Jesus.

Warm Regards From Your Prayer Cheerleader,
Rosetta

## FIRST THINGS FIRST

We humans all live in a physical, material world. Yet to become victorious Christians, we are called to believe in, relate to, and rely on a spiritual Supreme Being, God, whom we can't see with our natural eyes. Nevertheless, He is real. God exists. He is alive and He is the real deal.

Not only is our God Jehovah real, He is systematic and highly organized and has a kingdom that He rules over complete with laws and accepted ways of doing things. God invites us to get to know Him and grow in our knowledge of Him through His son, Jesus Christ.

The first building block to getting prayers answered and living an overall abundant life is to believe in your heart that Jesus Christ is one with God and that He is the mediator between God and Man. In order for you to truly access God, you have to go through Jesus. You must verbally acknowledge your need for Him and request that He grant you the new spiritual birth experience.

No matter what our level of understanding of spiritual things are, we won't go any higher unless we acknowledge His existence, our continued need for Him and then set out to draw closer to Him to learn more about the reality of His existence with the Holy Spirit's help.

We do this by asking to be born anew in our spirit man (also known as repenting), asking Him into our hearts to be Lord of our lives and walking daily with Him. That's what being a Born-Again Christian is all about. Please read Mark 1: 14-15 NIV and note the underlined emphasis on the kingdom of God. We will deal more with the topic of the Kingdom of God in Chapter 4.

> [14] After John was put in prison, Jesus went into Galilee, proclaiming the good news of God. [15] "The time has come," he said. "*The Kingdom of God* has come near. Repent and believe the good news!" (Mark 1:14-15, NIV)

and

> [3] Now there was a Pharisee, a man named Nicodemus who was a member of the Jewish ruling council. [2] He came to Jesus at night and said, "Rabbi, we know that you are a teacher who has come from God. For no one could perform the signs you are doing if God were not with him." [3] Jesus replied, "Very truly I tell you, no one can see *the Kingdom of God* unless they are born again." [4] "How can someone be born when they are old?" Nicodemus asked. "Surely they cannot enter a second time into their mother's womb to be born!" [5] Jesus answered, "Very truly I tell you, no one can enter the Kingdom of God unless they are born of water and the Spirit. [6] Flesh gives birth to flesh, but the Spirit gives birth to spirit." (John 3:1-6, NIV).

The revelations and truths that will be shared in this book are simply going to fly over your head if you haven't accepted Jesus Christ into your heart and asked to be born again. This is because you will be attempting to grasp spiritual concepts with your mind, which is still part of the flesh and is at enmity with all things spiritual including the knowledge of Christ as explained below:

> [5] Those who live according to the flesh have their minds set on what the flesh desires; but those who live in accordance with the Spirit have their minds set on what the Spirit desires. [6] The mind governed by the flesh is death, but the mind governed by the Spirit is life and peace. [7] The mind governed by the flesh is hostile to God; it does not submit to God's law, nor can it do so. [8] Those who

*Introduction*

are in the realm of the flesh cannot please God. (Romans 8:5–8, NIV)

It isn't till we become born again that our spirits are come alive and we are enabled to grasp spiritual truths. And even that first step, being born again, is not an automatic entry that makes it immediately possible for us to understand and learn the things of God. It takes deliberately praying and renewing our minds in Christ by feeding our spirits with the Word of God, which Jesus describes as life.

> ⁶³ The Spirit gives life; the flesh counts for nothing. The words I have spoken to you—they are full of the Spirit and life. (John 6:63, NIV)

If you aren't sure of your relationship or status with God, unsure of whether or not you have ever actually asked to be born again, or if you are in right standing with God, this is a wonderful time to ask the Lord for a fresh start in Him. Simply pray these words out loud:

"Heavenly Father, I ask for the new spiritual birth so I can be born again. Please forgive me of all my sins. Create in me a clean heart and equip me with everything I need so that I can enter and remain in your Kingdom. Amen."

Now that we have taken the steps to be translated into the Kingdom of God, we are now in a position to expect for God to hear us when we pray and we can move on into learning the key building blocks and strategies for prevailing prayer.

# CHAPTER 1

# PITIFUL TO POWERFUL

*God raises the poor from the dust and lifts the needy from the ash heap; He seats them with princes and has them inherit a throne of honor. 1 Samuel 2:8 (NIV)*

*Abba Father, I am here to start this transformational journey with you. I pray that you equip me with everything I need: mindset, strategy, perseverance etc. to allow you to successfully perfect what you are starting in and with me. Amen.*

Picture this scenario:

You are starting from scratch, building a new life because you had to cut ties with everything and everyone familiar to you. That's the sugar-coated version of your situation. Actually, you are on the run from your family because you totally cheated your brother out of his inheritance and he wants to kill you. You are not a perfect person, but you have made your peace with God. It's not like you have much of a choice: you are in the middle of nowhere, afraid of your brother and utterly terrified of being killed. So, you desperately call out to God for help, protection, and guidance. The Almighty hears your cries and shows up in your life big time, assuring you He will take care of you and eventually take you back home. You are grateful that in spite of your mess, God has given you a second chance.

With this promise in your back pocket, and a new pep in your step, you continue with your journey. You are looking for safety and respite from your troubles, and thankfully end up in your mom's brother's house. Your uncle happily takes you in, where for the next twenty years, your beautifully imagined future turns into the worst possible nightmare. You agree to seven years of servitude in order to marry the woman you love, but then your uncle does a switch-a-roo and tricks you into first marrying a woman you aren't even attracted to. Then, you have to work another seven years to pay off the dowry for the ability to marry your true love.

If your marital life isn't complicated enough, you are also subjected to unfair work practices, abuse, control, cheating and eventually, rejection, and jealousy. All this happens while working tirelessly for your uncle and with your best faith efforts. Unthinkable!

Imagine negotiating a salary, upon which you plan your life and expenses, only for your boss to keep changing the agreed upon amount at the last minute. This forever jeopardizes your best-laid plans to save and do normal things like regular progressive people do like saving, buying a home and getting ahead! But somehow, your life never settles down enough to give you some degree of regularity and normalcy. Something in your life is always out of control. Specifically, it is out of <u>Your</u> control. Everything you have, the comfort of your wives and kids, are all connected to your uncle, the bully. He is in control of the family, property, herds, and wealth. He can snatch them away from you in a moment's notice if you try to leave. Worse still, even if he does let you all go, you can't go back home because your brother's still out there, waiting to take you out! You feel stuck in life. And it's not just a feeling, it's a living reality. There's no other way of putting it; You ARE stuck between a rock and a hard place!

You wonder: "Where is the God who promised to take care of me?" "Why is He allowing this to happen to me?" "How could my life go so impossibly wrong when I know that I had the glorious encounter with God and He gave me His promise to take care of me and bring me safely back home?" You frequently try to push all those thoughts away and bravely try to make the best of your situation. But the gnawing thoughts resurface. Somewhere deep within you, just know this isn't quite the path of destiny you were supposed to be following, or the life you were originally intended to be living. This new parallel universe chafes like brand new shoes that never quite seem to break in. The chafing is rubbing you raw even as you fight back the tears and refuse to allow your frustration and discontent to overwhelm you. What is the way out of this existence and how do you ever get out of it all, still sane and actually victorious? Is that even within the realm of possibility?

This is the story of your so-called life, up until this point. If it sounds familiar it's because many people are going through similar life experiences, being dragged around by circumstances and situations, forever victimized by things that lie outside the scope of their control or authority.

This illustration is modeled off the true story of Jacob, son of Isaac, grandson of Abraham found in Genesis. Jacob was the younger of a set of twins, but before their birth it had been prophesied that he Jacob would ultimately be greater than his older twin brother Esau. As an adult, Jacob successfully schemed his way into defrauding his brother out of his rightful inheritance, thereby rightfully provoking Esau's ire and thirst for revenge. Jacob consequently has been on the run ever since. He takes refuge in his uncle's home, in a strange land where they didn't serve the true and living God and works for him to regain his footing and rebuild his own life. But his dreams and aspirations are seemingly being thwarted by several events that have him bound in a place of great difficulty in every aspect of life.

Here are Jacob's exact words as he is describing his ordeal to his wife Rachel and his uncle/father-in-law, Laban:

> [6] You know that I've worked for your father with all my strength, [7] yet your father has cheated me by changing my wages ten times. However, God has not allowed him to harm me. (Gen. 30:6, NIV).

> [38] "I have been with you (Laban) for twenty years now. Your sheep and goats have not miscarried, nor have I eaten rams from your flocks. [39] I did not bring you animals torn by wild beasts; I bore the loss myself. And you demanded payment from me for whatever was stolen by day or night. [40] This was my situation: The heat consumed me in the daytime and the cold at night, and sleep fled from my eyes. [41] It was like this for the twenty years I was in your household. I worked for you fourteen years for your two daughters and six years for your flocks, and you changed my wages ten times. [42] If the God of my father, the God of Abraham and the Fear of Isaac, had not been with me, you would surely have sent me away empty-handed. But God has seen my hardship and the toil of my hands, and last night he rebuked you."
> (Gen. 31: 38-42, NIV)

Let's take a closer look at the situation Jacob finds himself in according the passage (Gen. 31:38-42). Jacob has been working as a shepherd for **twenty years**, and his Uncle Laban has unfairly changed the terms of Jacob's employment ten times! (Can you imagine hearing at the end of your regular two-week work period that your hourly pay rate dropped from say $10 an hour to $8 an hour? And this happened more than once, even as you continued to loyally put in quality work?) Wouldn't it be frustrating to think all your hard work is going to build an evil man's wealth? Jacob worked hard to take care of Laban's flocks, and made up for any loss out of his own pocket.

For twenty years, Jacob worked exposed to the elements: long, hot days and freezing temperatures at night. Jacob worked hard in order to earn his fiancee's dowry, but was tricked into marrying a woman he didn't want. Then he had to work even longer so he could pay off the dowry to marry the love of his life.

Yet, through it all, God is working in, with, and for Jacob. Slowly, he manages to turn the tables on his nemesis and gain the upper hand. Jacob's life is transformed from victim to victor! He is no longer the broke but dedicated shepherd of his uncle Laban's sheep. God enables Jacob to become a far wealthier man (in his own right) than Laban ever was, while still working for him! Imagine being Laban's shepherd or hired help, but you are your own wealthy man, complete with your own flocks, servants, camels, and donkeys. The servant now has his own servants. (Gen. 30:43) Talk about a reversal of fortune!

What happened that catapulted Jacob from being a servant to being exceedingly prosperous, until his uncle and his sons were jealous and resentful of him (as seen in Gen. 31:1-2)? It's obvious that Jacob became so powerful his uncle could no longer control him like he used to. Many such examples of complete turn-around situations abound in the Word of God. How does this kind of change happen? What lessons can we take from this and other stories in the Bible that will allow us to overturn seemingly impossible situations, be delivered from oppression, sickness and all kinds of unimaginable problems and bondages, as well as experience reconciliation?

## PREVAILING PRAYER

The answer to all these questions and any other conundrum in life you might face is PRAYER. Not just any type of prayer, but PREVAILING PRAYER. So, what is prevailing prayer? According to dictionary.com, the word "prevail" means all of the following:

1. to be or prove superior in strength, power, or influence (usually followed by *over*),
2. to succeed; become dominant; win out:
3. to use persuasion or inducement successfully:

In effect, prevailing prayer will enable us to prove superior in strength, power, and influence over the natural order of this world, our own selves and the Devil, using not our own power but God's power. Prevailing prayer will tap into the Biblical keys that will allow us to become spiritually successful, to gain the upper hand and to be winners. Prevailing prayer will show us how to pray successfully with persuasion, presenting our case before the Lord and productively reasoning with Him on why He should answer our prayers.

Prevailing prayer changes people, situations, and things (both natural and spiritual) by enforcing God's mind, Word, and Will to manifest in the earth realm. Prevailing prayer affects change. Prevailing prayer is prayer that overcomes our circumstances by super-imposing or enforcing God's will over the natural order or progression of the world. It is operative. Prevailing prayer causes supernatural things to manifest in the earth realm. Prevailing prayer is productive and brings results. For example, the prophet Elijah was a powerful prayer warrior. The Bible says: "The prayer of a righteous person is powerful and effective. Elijah was a human being, even as we are. He prayed earnestly that it would not rain, and it did not rain on the land for three and a half years. Again he prayed, and the heavens gave rain, and the earth produced its crops" (James 5:16B – 17, NIV).

Dear Friend, these things I am describing are well within the realm of possibility and there are many everyday Christians whose lives are living proof of the reality of prevailing prayer. As we will discover over the course of this book, the Bible provides many clues on how to tap into the open secrets of prevailing prayer. We will learn the fundamental principles needed to have a prevailing prayer life and we will examine the lives of ordinary people who were able to prevail over their various circumstances, just as Jacob did.

Jacob's story resonates deeply within me in many ways. The instability of his life has a very familiar ring to it. It's a life that somehow seems to be just beyond the reach of predictability and control, with one unforeseen circumstance right on the heels of another. About ten years ago, my life seemed to be a series of unending troubles with a parade of defeats, delays, denials, disappointments, and disillusionments.

Have you ever been in a position where you were really between a rock and a ridiculously hard place? A place where things felt beyond your control? I can really identify with Jacob's position of feeling pitiful and powerless. In my case, it wasn't for lack of trying to change my circumstances, but all my efforts were seemingly stymied. I previously worked as a career coach and among other things, I wrote effective resumes that helped many people reach their career goals. I counseled and helped them implement strategies how to get ahead in their careers. But when it came to me, I couldn't get anywhere. I must have re-written eight versions of my own resumes with great cover letters and put in dozens of job applications. I typically never got called in for interviews. When I did get calls, they were from direct referrals because people I knew had personally asked for me by name because of the quality of work I had delivered when I had worked with them before.

I remember being disappointed in God. I felt I had given Him my all, tried to serve Him the very best I could, with the sincerest and purest heart. Wasn't I obedient? I thought that if I delighted myself in the Lord He would give me the desires of my heart (Psalm 37:4). I had worked hard! With His help, I had a bachelor's degree from a great school but was chronically under-employed or unemployed. How could God keep allowing me to get laid off (again and again) from my corporate HR jobs in recruiting, career coaching, training, and development? How come it always seemed to take me so long to find my next gig? When I did find something and I was working, I could only find a contractor gig, with no paid time off, no vacation, no benefits. I was sometimes asked to work less than forty hours a week because my employer was also struggling. I was always broke and couldn't seem to find the ends anywhere, much less try to make those ends meet.

Coupled with all these professional problems, my home front was also under siege. (Don't even get me started on all the marital drama Jacob went through and the in-fighting between his two sister wives, Leah and Rachel!) While I was anxious about my inconsistent work life and the ensuing financial problems, my husband who didn't share the same hang-ups I had about money didn't seem to be in the least bit deterred from spending. I was just one anxious, nervous wreck all the time!

It didn't help that my husband and I just didn't get along. (Now that's a major understatement!) We could barely stand one another. We argued frequently over everything and nothing. For all intents and purposes, we were literally irreconcilably different. I was emotionally drained all the time because I was constantly mentally playing out all the different ways to get back at him. It was either that or I was working up my energies, preparing for the next round of arguments that I refused to lose. I did all this while silently screaming out to God for help in a million different ways. I was like the guy in the cell phone commercial who travels to many different locations with cell phone towers, cell phone pressed to his ear asking the same incessant question: "Can you hear me now? Can you hear me now?" Well, that was the story of my life, and I know there are many other Christians bravely going through these same motions saying: "Are you out there? God…? Somebody…?, Anybody…?"

I worked harder in my marriage. I wanted to communicate more effectively and be less confrontational. I was striving to be the "perfect" Christian wife hologram and I was comparing myself to the people at church who made a healthy relationship look so effortless. But I couldn't live up to those expectations, no matter how hard I tried. I was just chafing in my own skin and hating every bit of it.

Oh, did I mention we had two small children too? I was a hot pitiful mess! My life was miserable and unraveling in slow motion, right before my eyes. I was powerless in my own strength to do anything about it.

None of the "good", even godly activities I had been practicing were in and of themselves enough to accomplish the kinds of breakthroughs and miracles I needed in my life. It wasn't enough to say "I am too blessed to be stressed." Platitudes like this didn't help me overcome my difficulties.

So began the quest to connect with God in a new way. I had always known and seen evidence of God working in my life as well as other people's lives. I knew that He was the Way, the Truth and the Life (John 14:6). Once things started falling apart, even though I initially blamed Him for my misfortunes (I thought God had abandoned me) I knew *I* was missing something. I started to diligently seek Him for answers. But it took a while to even grasp that there is no true substitute for focused, deliberate, results-oriented prayer. Just hoping for the best wasn't going to cut it. Just formulating my best laid plans with no actual input from God wasn't enough to get me where I needed to be. Asking others to pray on my behalf and reading quick fly-by prayers on Facebook that commanded me to type AMEN were grossly inadequate and getting me nowhere.

I temporarily moved away from my marital home while I tried to get some answers from God. I could have lost my marriage during that separation and to be honest, I wasn't sure if I cared. But the more I sought the Lord for His mind and His will (not just my personal preference for my comfort, or to accommodate my husband's pleas that we stay married) the more I felt impressed upon that He wanted a reconciliation for my marriage. He would make a way for us to live a more victorious Christian marriage. The Lord showed me Scripture verses promising that He would make a way in the wilderness for us, that He would restore what the locust and cankerworm had eaten (Joel 2:25). (Remember, God is in the business of healing!)

Over time, the Lord gave me the will to fight for a renewed marriage. I went from being indifferent to caring. I began to realize that as a faithful child of God who had always strived to live right, the enemy of my soul simply didn't want to see me fulfilled in marriage and life in general. I was in a major battle and I wasn't going to concede without a fight! There was no way I was going to throw my marriage away; I had prayed and waited too long for God to send this man for me to just give up. Was I to allow our problems to overshadow everything else and concede another defeat in my life? Absolutely not!

In order for this marriage to be saved, God had to perform the greatest miracle in both of our personalities. For me, He would have to change me: my heart, my temper, and give me control over my tongue. I also had to relinquish control and patiently look to God to work in my husband's heart! I had no recourse but to trust God that things were going to change and that somehow we would eventually live in victory, if we were going to be reconciled.

God gave me the grace to continue to pray earnestly about His promises for me and my family, and honestly about my fears, casting my burdens onto Him (1 Peter 5:7). It took many leaps of faith, each of which essentially still involved the same steps Jacob went through. God worked separately in our hearts, came through for us individually, and then as a couple. He then restored us, to the glory of His name, and continues to work within us to grow from where we started. There has been no magic wand, just lots of willingness to question and seek, to go back to the drawing board and pray. It has also included lots of willful decisions to obey and trust God in spite of my feelings and rationalizing and to submit myself to Him and my husband, even when it hasn't been the most pleasurable thing to do. But even as I have attempted to stay close to God, I have seen such incredible spiritual changes in me. The seemingly messy and difficult areas of my life have only been fertilizer that has driven me to my knees and into the Word so I can continue to overcome and reign with Him.

## Mess to Message

Now that the Lord has taught me enough to be dangerous, after implementing and seeing the fruit of my labors and the manifold joys and benefits prayer brings, I know I can't keep fellow Christians in the dark. I have to share what I have learned! I know it will make all the difference in the world.

## Thoughts and Tips on Prayer Execution

1. "Blessed are those who hunger and thirst after righteousness for they shall be filled." (Matt. 5:6, NIV). Are you truly hungry for a change in your spiritual and physical conditions? People will undergo painful surgical procedures just to see a change in their physical appearance. Your transformation will also entail some discomfort. How do you plan on bracing for it?
2. Truly hungry people—starving is a better word—will do desperate things to stay alive. Do you want to truly be alive in Christ? If God wanted you to demonstrate your hunger for Him, how would you go about making that happen? Really pause to think about what actionable item you would take. How do you increase your hunger for God?

## PRAYER POINTS

In closing this chapter, we will employ some prayer points culled from the verses and topics we have discussed to seal the application of the concepts introduced.

These prayer points are to be prayed meditatively, preferably out loud and repeatedly until you feel a release to move on. There is no magic formula, but do ask the Holy Spirit to help you to pray in accordance with what He knows you need. He will often use a prayer point as a base to bring something else to the forefront of your mind to be tackled in prayer. Let us pray!

- ❖ Father, you know everything that concerns me: my prayers, my fears, my needs, wants, and desires. I lift everything that concerns me into your most capable hands. I choose to walk with you, Lord, and not by myself. I draw near to you, Father and I thank you for drawing near to me. Make me more aware of this process of being drawn closer to you.
- ❖ I pray that you enable me to partner with you for my life to become a breeding ground for turnarounds, breakthroughs, miracles, signs, wonders, even as you did for Jacob and many others.
- ❖ Lord, help me to actively seek you for a more effective prayer life so I can understand and fulfill my purpose. I declare in Jesus' mighty name that I will attain many great results and rewards as we move forward together. Thank you, Holy Spirit for maximum results in my prayer life.
- ❖ Holy Spirit, show me how to diligently monitor my feelings, thought life and circumstances that I face and to talk to you about everything.
- ❖ Holy Spirit, empower me to recognize every time I am being railroaded by arguments, distractions, and any other tricks of the enemy so I can effectively deal with them.
- ❖ By the power in the blood and name of Jesus, I destroy every weapon fashioned against me, and anything attempting to stymie my spiritual growth.

- ❖ I silence every voice talking me out of a stronger relationship with God and more effective prayer life in the name of the Lord Jesus Christ.
- ❖ Anything in my life that like Laban is thwarting my best efforts to move ahead, let its power be destroyed in the name of Jesus.
- ❖ In Jesus' name let the spirit of the emptier that would love to send me away empty-handed in spite of all my hard work be disgraced.
- ❖ Anything devouring stability, peace, progress, joy, and any of the blessings that are part of my covenant rights as a child of God, let their tables be overturned. Father, let them not have dominion in my life in Jesus' name.
- ❖ Lord, anything stealing from me, destroying or attempting to kill me and good things concerning me, whether spiritually or physically, I pray for their destruction. I pray that their grip on my life will be loosened so I can be free from their oppression.
- ❖ Father, I pray in Jesus' name that you will re-arrange circumstances in my life so I can live that victorious, more abundant life that Jesus promised me in John 10:10.

# CHAPTER 2

# PLATFORM FOR PREVAILING PRAYER

*Prayer is the easiest and hardest of all things; the simplest and the sublimest; the weakest and the most powerful; its results lie outside the range of human possibilities-they are limited only by the omnipotence of God. – E.M. Bounds*

*My Heavenly Father, open my spirit to access the revelational knowledge in your Word that will provide your answers to my questions. I ask for the grace to react obediently to what you tell. I choose to cooperate with you all the way to the finish line and not abort the process that will take me to a manifestation of my desires. In Jesus' name, Amen.*

We have already discussed with prevailing prayer means but let's go back and first address what exactly constitutes prayer itself in the Christian tradition.

## WHAT IS PRAYER?

In its simplest terms, prayer is a system of talking to God. It is a communication system between man and God made up of talking and listening on both sides, with the Word of God as the intermediary between the two parties. I refer to this as traditional three-dimensional prayer. This three-way communication system is essentially captured in this ditty that you probably sang yourself as a child:

> "Read your Bible, pray every day, pray every day, pray every day. Read your Bible, pray every day if you want to grow."

As illustrated on the right side of this triangular diagram below, man talks to God in prayer, and our goal is for God to respond to us, however He chooses. There are a variety of ways He uses: sometimes He talks directly back to His children, in other instances He introduces thoughts into our minds or impresses feelings into our hearts; often He communicates by speaking through others and also, by arranging circumstances in such a way that we get answered prayer. God also talks to us through dreams and visions, etc.

We also see from the left side of the picture that God talks to man through the scriptures, as represented by the arrow going down from God to scriptures. As we seek our heavenly creator by feasting on the Word, (arrow going from scripture to man) we are better able to understand and trust God's mind and character as revealed in His Word. As we grow in this area, our faith grows, our spirits mature, and we become more emboldened. Our prayers become more effective as we give His revealed words back to Him in prayer (arrow going from man back to scripture and back up to God.) We do this because we recognize that God is bound by His word to act on His Word concerning our prayer requests. The more exposure to the Word and will of God we have, the more aligned we become with Him and the more likely we are to get our prayers answered.

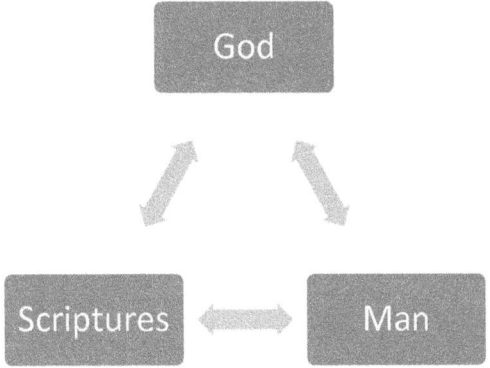

In light of this diagram, let us re-examine the story of Jacob which we started out in the introduction of this book with. I proposed that Jacob had an active prayer life which was the foundation of the changes he experienced in his life. There are some clues about Jacob's life specifically in Genesis 28, 30, 31, and 32 which point to evidence of Jacob having an effective prayer life. The following three things had a significant role in his transformation:

1. The Word/ promises of God,
2. Jacob's response to the promises and
3. Obedience to God's Word.

Let's examine each of these:

## 1. THE WORD/PROMISES OF GOD

We see here that while fleeing to his uncle's house God spoke to Jacob in a dream and gave him a promise:

> ¹² He had a dream in which he saw a stairway resting on the earth, with its top reaching to heaven, and the angels of God were ascending and descending on it. ¹³ There above it[c] stood the LORD, and he said: "I am the LORD, the God of your father Abraham and the God of Isaac. I will give you and your descendants the land on which you are lying. ¹⁴ Your descendants will be like the dust

of the earth, and you will spread out to the west and to the east, to the north and to the south. All peoples on earth will be blessed through you and your offspring.[15] I am with you and will watch over you wherever you go, and I will bring you back to this land. I will not leave you until I have done what I have promised you." (Gen 28:12-15, NIV).

God recognized the distress Jacob was in and promised him He would be protected and eventually brought safely back to his home. This is an example of God speaking directly to man; in this case, it happened through a dream. This is symbolized by the arrow pointing directly from God to man.

It must be pointed out at this juncture that God routinely continues to speak to people in their dreams, and as you seek the Lord and your prayer life develops, you should be examining your dreams more closely because God will often talk to you in your dreams. God continues to reveal Himself to us in His word, even if it isn't always in as dramatic a fashion as Jacob's dream was. Every day, He is tugging on us to draw closer, inviting us a deeper walk, telling us He will be with us no matter what but we all still have a choice to make, a response to give to His call.

The essence of the Word of God and its centrality to our prayer life can't possibly be overstated. There is no Christianity without the Word of God and we will have no real success or staying power in prayer without it as a foundation to our faith walk. The Bible exhorts us many times to consume the Word and incorporate it into our lives because it is a sword, with which we fight the enemy. Unfortunately, the average Christian is sorely lacking in knowledge of the Word and so we frequently lose battles we should handily win. Not knowing the Word is like going into a battle unprepared; it decreases our chances of winning or even coming out alive.

Given that the Bible is a huge and somewhat confusing book, it is quite daunting a task for a lay person to immediately find and understand suitable verses within the right context, that are applicable to one's specific situation. This is why many of my clients are drawn to the prayer consultations my prayer team offers. Pray, Slay and Reign's Prayer consultations help Believers more effectively identify the foundational issues behind your problems that need to be addressed in prayer. We cut through the confusion of you personally trying to navigate the Bible and figure out what specific verses are relevant to your problems before you do the actual work of praying the Word. Prayer consultations facilitate a quicker process of establishing an effective battle plan.

Let's now look at how Jacob's transformation journey evolved.

## 2. JACOB'S RESPONSE TO THE PROMISE

Jacob had a choice to make after this incredible encounter and that response is in itself a form of obedience to God. We see Jacob replied by in turn, giving God a promise, or a vow, almost like a promissory ring. This prayer is represented by the arrow going from man back up to God.

> [20] Then Jacob made a vow, saying, "If God will be with me and will watch over me on this journey I am taking and will give me food to eat and clothes to wear [21] so that I return safely to my father's household, then the LORD[f] will be my God [22] and[g] this stone that I have set up as a pillar will be God's house, and of all that you give me I will give you a tenth." (Gen 28:20-22, NIV).

While Jacob's promise sounds quite self-serving to me, it is still honest and it is a start in the right direction. He and God struck a deal and it was now up to both sides to honor their parts of their deal, come sunshine or rain. Jacob continued his journey and went on to find and live with his uncle. He went through several incredibly trying years at the hands of his uncle. I believe that despite his terribly challenging work troubles and personal life situations (how would you like to be married to two dueling sisters, one of whom you didn't even ever express interest in!) Jacob stood on God's promise to never leave him and to watch over him. As crushingly difficult as his circumstances were, Jacob kept God's Word alive in Him because he knew that since the self-existing, never-ending God was on His side, he Jacob would eventually make it out of his predicament.

How do we keep the Word God gives us alive? We keep it in hearts by meditating on it and on our lips by verbalizing or speaking it out.

> **2** My son, if you accept my words and store up my commands within you...⁵ then you will understand the fear of the Lord and find the knowledge of God.⁶ For the Lord gives wisdom; from his mouth come knowledge and understanding.⁷ *He holds success in store for the upright*, he is a shield to those whose walk is blameless,⁸ for he guards the course of the just and protects the way of his faithful ones. (Prov. 2:1, 5-7, NIV).

> ⁸ This book of the law shall not depart out of thy mouth; but thou shalt meditate therein day and night, that thou mayest observe to do according to all that is written therein: for then thou shalt make thy way prosperous, and *then thou shalt have good success.* (Josh. 1:8, KJV).

These verses are exciting to me because there is a clear promise of success attached to our correct response to the Word of God. In the second passage, God tells Joshua if you will continue to let my Words be part of your speech, if you don't stop verbalizing my words, you will have good success. The first likewise, encourages us to accept and store up God's commands so we can enjoy the many benefits of our relationship with God, which includes protection, security, knowledge, understanding, and success. Success is literally inevitable if we do what God tells us to do!

When we go back to the diagram we see that by rehearsing that divine Word in his spirit and making it his own reality by (represented by the horizontal arrow going from scriptures to man and vice versa) and then speaking it back up to God in prayer (arrow goes from scripture back to God). In due season, God answered Jacob's prayer with very specific instructions (arrow goes from God back down to man) on how to outwit his uncle and create his own personal wealth:

> [10] "In breeding season I once had a dream in which I looked up and saw that the male goats mating with the flock were streaked, speckled or spotted. [11] The angel of God said to me in the dream, 'Jacob.' I answered, 'Here I am.' [12] And he said, 'Look up and see that all the male goats mating with the flock are streaked, speckled or spotted, for I have seen all that Laban has been doing to you. [13] I am the God of Bethel, where you anointed a pillar and where you made a vow to me. (Gen. 31:10-13a, NIV).

So, as we can see from this example, the cycle continues and Jacob goes from one mountain of glory to another, and from one level of faith to another. This is his second recorded encounter with God and this time, he is empowered to bring about the change and way out that he has been so desperately seeking. But the story doesn't stop there; if Jacob had not followed through with his instructions, he would still have been held under his uncle's oppressive rule. Thus, step three is critical to seeing the results of one's prayer.

So, to recap this section, upon being confronted by the Word of God, our first response is to give it the proper environment so it can take root and grow in our hearts. We first acknowledge and then ingest that Word or promise so that it becomes part of our psyche and belief system. This type of obedience is really all about first accepting and believing in what God reveals of Himself by the promises or Words he speaks to us.

## 3. Obedience to God's Word

Genesis 30:25-42 goes into great detail on the strategy and the plan of execution Jacob utilized to get his end results after receiving revelation from God in his second dream about mating livestock on the way forward. Jacob could have gone through all the motions of receiving the Word from God, meditating on, standing on, and praying/speaking the Word back to God and still been left in the same predicament if he hasn't been obedient to the latter instructions and revelations God gave him. This is especially true since God's strategy He revealed to Jacob was quite unconventional.

Way before the scientific knowledge of genetics was discovered, God gave Jacob a revelation on dominant and recessive genes, and visualization, both of which he skillfully used to exponentially increase his livestock until no matter what trickery his uncle Laban pulled, Jacob still had the upper hand.

Look at Solomon's words about some of the benefits of accepting and embracing the Word of God:

> [12] Wisdom will save you from the ways of wicked men, from men whose words are perverse,[13] who have left the straight paths to walk in dark ways,[14] who delight in doing wrong and rejoice in the perverseness of evil,[15] whose paths are crooked and who are devious in their ways. (Prov. 2:12-15, NIV).

Your problems may or may not be directly orchestrated by actual evil people. It is possible they are demonically inspired, as Job's problems were. Whatever the origin of your problems, God can still give you the keys to overthrow that very real evil agenda and ensuing activities that are militating against you however you still have to go through all these three steps as outlined above.

Many Christians today will not obey God because what He tells them to do may seem outlandish, just as God's visualization strategy to tie sticks by the pool where Jacob's livestock were mating was outlandish. The instructions He gave Jacob were surely bizarre by anyone's standard. But it didn't deter Jacob from obeying. Jacob ultimately achieved his success by learning God's divine plan for and promise to him. He then appropriated that word for himself and made it his reality by meditating on it and then praying it back to God, while asking for a way out. Eventually, God spoke to him again and gave him a game plan, which he then followed and executed on and then he got his desired results. This is often the path God takes with His children. It is our responsibility to be diligent in seeking, sober, and alert in hearing and faithful in obeying. These are the fundamental components of a prevailing prayer life and none of the steps in the process can be compromised if we want to see our God move on our behalf with answered prayers.

*Platform for Prevailing Prayer*

I must add here as a side note that this traditional illustration of prayer doesn't take into account the real existence of evil, embodied by Satan and His fallen angels, their activities against us Believers, and our response back to their activities (known as spiritual warfare.) The truth of the matter is that no truly victorious or prevailing prayer lifestyle will be complete or sustainable in the absence of spiritual warfare. Therefore, a more accurate depiction of prevailing prayer looks more like the picture below:

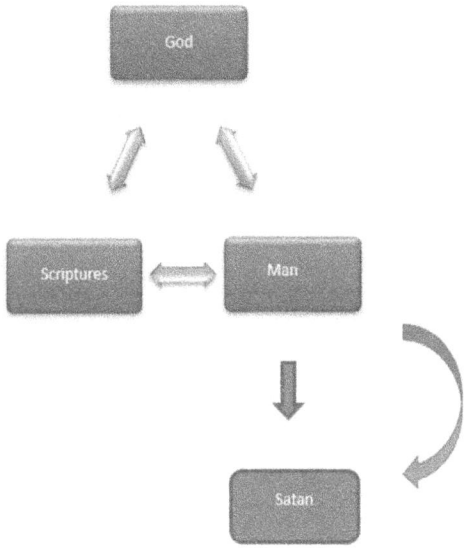

The added elements to this prayer equation are the kingdom of darkness represented by Satan and positioned under the Believer's feet (Rom. 16:20 and Gen. 3:15) and the curved arrow from man to Satan. The latter refers to the means by which we keep him in that position where he is subdued under our feet. After all, thanks to Jesus, we are superior to him as chapter 7, Christ in Me the Hope of Glory shows us. There are many ways and weapons by which we keep the enemy under our feet so we win out or prevail over him. Especially in chapter 5 Kingdom Keys for Prevailing Prayer, chapter 9 Enter the Dragon and chapter 10 The Practice of Prevailing Prayer we gain a more complete understanding of how to keep our enemy subdued under our feet.

## My first personal rescue encounter with God

One of my very first personal encounters with God I recollect took place sometime when I was thirteen. I remember being home on holidays from boarding school and feeling slightly unwell that day. I retired to my room early that evening but continued to deteriorate. I remember being very uneasy but I couldn't quite pinpoint what exactly was wrong. It was a great malaise of spirit, more so than a physical ailment. Whatever was initially wrong was soon eclipsed by a very urgent and real premonition that something was terribly wrong. As I lay tossing in my bed an almost audible taunt tore through my spirit: "You are going to die tonight!" It felt as real as my own hand in front of my face. The room's walls felt like they were closing in on me and I just knew it was literally my last night on earth as what felt like a cacophony of hellish sounds jeered and taunted that I was going to Hell that night.

I was a fairly new babe in Christ at that point but I knew there were some areas of my life that weren't fully under Christ's control so I just knew those demons were right and I was not going to make it to Heaven. But I was too discomfited to think or pray coherently but I just knew I wasn't going to be alive the next morning. Imagine not being able to say goodbye to your family, but knowing this was going to be the last time you ever saw them on earth. I came from a very rational and scientific family. There was no way they were going to believe me. I didn't even know how to begin to explain what I was feeling to my parents. On top of it all, they weren't even born again so they wouldn't understand. So, I suffered in my room alone with my thoughts and the very real demonic oppression in my room that night. I distinctly recollect staring at the brown wood veneered doors of the built-in closets in that room that night, looking at my mom's neatly stacked suitcases on top of the wardrobe and thinking this would be the last thing I saw on earth before going to Heaven.

By some act of grace, my little sister came and sat by me to comfort me but I couldn't really tell her what was going on in my heart. She graciously offered to bring me my Good News Bible. At first, I just cradled it, unsure where to go. I knew I needed a word from God but was too frozen by fear to even think straight or know where to go. Well, as soon as my sister said good night and left my room, I just flipped the bible open and the Holy Spirit immediately caused it to open to Isaiah 43 where the following words leaped off the page and into my spirit:

> **43** Israel, the LORD who created you says, *"Do not be afraid—I will save you.* I have called you by name—you are mine.[2] When you pass through deep waters, I will be with you; your troubles will not overwhelm you. *When you pass through fire, you will not be burned;* the hard trials that come will not hurt you.[3] For I am the LORD your God, the holy God of Israel, who saves you, I will give up Egypt to set you free; I will give up Ethiopia[a] and Seba.[4] I will give up whole nations to save your life, because you are precious to me and because I love you and give you honor. [5] *Do not be afraid—I am with you!* (Is. 43:1-5, GNT).

Oh, what comfort these words brought to me! For years after this incident this was my favorite scripture. I latched onto the words "Do not be afraid… I will be with you. Do not be afraid, I am with you", and its light flooded my spirit and soul. I was able to pray and ask the Lord to take me home to be with Him when I died (I didn't have faith to ask for my life to be spared at that point.) I fell asleep repeating to myself "Do not be afraid, I will be with you", a little like Dorothy in the Wizard of Oz did, repeating follow the yellow brick road.

I was shocked to find myself still on earth the next morning when I woke up. What I had encountered the night before was so real, I was sure I had died and gone to Heaven in my sleep. I remember hearing our house help Alli crying loudly outside and bringing me to consciousness and me thinking "There's no crying or weeping in Heaven. What's going on here? I thought I was supposed to be going to Heaven!"

I groggily made my way out of the room, down the narrow hallway, past the kitchen door where Alli was weeping loudly. I asked what was wrong and she led me to the formal living room area where

I discovered to my astonishment that the house had caught fire the night before, consumed a portion of the room from floor to ceiling and then mysteriously died out by itself! I still get chills when I replay that scene in my mind. Alli had not properly disposed of a coal pot full of charcoal embers and had inadvertently started the fire right behind the living room that evening when I wasn't feeling well and had the premonition of dying. The position of my room in the layout of the home was such that I would have been the first casualty if the fire had spread past the living room. I would have been trapped as there was no back door for me to have escaped out of.

As for the actual scene of the fire in the living room itself, it was a clear miracle and obvious that an angel of God had intervened and squelched the fierce blaze! Mom's beautiful curtains and drapery were completely incinerated and the only traces of their existence was an eerie angel wing shaped silhouette on the walls where they used to be. The fire burned from the base of the wall where the hot coal embers had been placed all the way to the wooden balustrade and ornate wood-paneled ceiling. The wood burned to a crisp and then extinguished completely by itself, all while we slept a few feet away. The heat from the fire was so strong that the metal louvre blades that held the glass slats had all warped and melted. The half-inch thick layer of cement plaster spackling on top of the cement bricks making up the inner and outer parts of the living room wall had buckled under the intensity of the flames and separated from the bricks beneath. The terrazzo floor on the inside and cemented floor of the backyard was still too hot to step on several hours after the fire and best of all, the electric wire of the standing fan right next to the window and partially covered by the now-burnt drapes had somehow melted but didn't itself burst into an electrical fire. It was just an amazing sight. No one heard anything or tried to intervene, but God surely kept His promise to me that even if I went through the fire, He would be there with me! Abba Father came through for me big time that day and our whole family rejoiced at God's great faithfulness of promise of protection to me.

As grateful as I am for this experience, I also know there can be a hidden danger in relying on these kinds of dramatic rescue situations as evidence of ability to have a prevailing life of prayer. It can get easy for us to assume that all we have to do as Christians is to only take God at His Word, rarely do anything else and see Him perform "bigly" on our behalf. Many Christians live most of their faith walk this way and assume we are always going to get answered prayer this way. It becomes easy to coast and do nothing to stoke our relationship with the Lord and then show up at His throne when there is a crisis, expecting Him to jump at our beck and call because we have an emergency.

This is not the permanent kind of relationship God wants to have with us and even if He is kind enough to come through for His children, it doesn't mean He is obliged to do so. If we His children deliberately neglect Him all the time or just minimally relate to Him in a very superficial way, and then come expecting miracles because of our sudden importunities, we run the risk of Him not coming through for us in our difficult times. We can become complacent if we adopt that kind of mindset. This mentality makes me cringe when I hear it reflected in songs that say things like "God will fight my battles if I just keep still" and use that verse as a license to do nothing at all, when God requires participation rather than spectatorship from us in our prayer lives.

## Who is Responsible For Prayer?

Many Christians in the twenty first century church are under the wrong impression that prayer is the work of a select few giants in the faith. Many say very sporadic and brief prayers to fulfill their Christian duty but know fully well that if they really want God to move, it most likely won't be on account of their personal ability to get their prayers through. Consequently, many Believers bank on a praying mom or grand-mom or call on everyone to pray for them when things are really difficult. These days there are loads of Facebook communities dedicated to praying for others. While this is a noble cause, ultimately, God wants each person to bear their own weight and responsibility in prayer.

Peter tells us that Christ redeemed us all to Himself so we can be his royal and holy priests:

> *You also, like living stones, are being built into a spiritual house to be a holy priesthood,* offering spiritual sacrifices acceptable to God through Jesus Christ… *But you* are a chosen people, *a royal priesthood,* a holy nation, God's special possession, that you may declare the praises of him who called you out of darkness into his wonderful light. (1 Peter 2:4, 9, NIV).

When the disciples asked Jesus to teach them to pray, his response was "*When* you pray say…" (Luke 11:22, KJV), not "*If* you pray…"

By the same token, it is recorded that:

> "He (Jesus) spake a parable unto them to this end, that men ought *always* to pray and not faint…" (Luke 18:1, KJV).

Even more importantly, we know that the greatest commandment for us as chosen Children of God is:

> [30] And thou shalt love the Lord thy God with all thy heart, and with all thy soul, and with all thy mind, and with all thy strength: this is the first commandment. (Mark 12:30, KJV)

Furthermore, Jesus states very clearly to His disciples and by extension, we the church that:

> [15] "If ye love me, keep my commandments." (John 14:15, KJV)

and that our love of God is evident by the keeping of His commandments which are not burdensome or grievous (1 John 5:3). As love and communication go together in the natural, so love and prayer flow together. In fact, I am going out on a limb here, daring to say that God expects you to love and express yourself to Him (pray) with all your heart (aka spirit), soul and mind. There is no such thing as humans loving God without fervent, engaged prayer. We are simply deceiving ourselves with anything less.

Many know we are required to pray but don't truly believe it will make a difference in our lives and so we don't see the need to pray. We mostly believe we are self-sufficient enough that we can make it on our own. We therefore don't ask for input from our Father in the seemingly mundane areas of our lives and only approach Him when things don't seem to be going our way. The truth of the matter is, we have all cried out in desperation to God for one thing or the other, only for nothing to have changed. We have had hopes dashed, or felt the stinging pain of defeat in prayer and consequently, threw in the towel or grew very lukewarm toward it all. Nevertheless, our Heavenly Father invites us to dialogue with Him and *promises* to hear us. Here are a few verses that prove my point.

> [11] For I know the thoughts that I think toward you, saith the LORD, thoughts of peace, and not of evil, to give you an expected end. [12] Then shall ye call upon me, and ye shall go and pray unto me, and I will hearken unto you. [13] *And ye shall seek me, and find me, when ye shall search for me with all your heart.* (Jer. 29:11-13, KJV) and

> [2] "This is what the LORD says, he who made the earth, the LORD who formed it and established it—the LORD is his name: [3] *'Call to me and I will answer you* and tell you great and unsearchable things you do not know.' (Jer. 33:2-3, NIV).

I love these promises because they speak clearly about God's invitation to us and His intent to make good on our efforts. They also express His clear delight in hearing from us. He sounds like a proud dad, happy to get a phone call from his beloved kids. I use these verses to remind God when I think He is silent or not moving quickly enough on my behalf (did I mention I am particularly impatient and prone to giving up? Yes, I like instant gratification!) Nevertheless, I am more perturbed by this parable Jesus told because

*Prevailing Prayer*

He is referring to His return and I think we are all guilty of possibly being the people He is talking about:

> **18** And he spake a parable unto them to this end, that men ought always to pray, and not to faint;² Saying, There was in a city a judge, which feared not God, neither regarded man:³ And there was a widow in that city; and she came unto him, saying, Avenge me of mine adversary.⁴ And he would not for a while: but afterward he said within himself, Though I fear not God, nor regard man;⁵ Yet because this widow troubleth me, I will avenge her, lest by her continual coming she weary me.⁶ And the Lord said, Hear what the unjust judge saith.⁷ And shall not God avenge his own elect, which cry day and night unto him, though he bear long with them? ⁸ I tell you that he will avenge them speedily. *Nevertheless when the Son of man cometh, shall he find faith on the earth?* (Luke 18:1-8, KJV)

In this story, we find that the person who needed their situation fixed waited long for a resolution, but eventually, God did indeed come through for her. However, Jesus' final question at the end really gives me pause. He wonders if when He returns, He will find people who have endured and who didn't give up after not seeing results for a while. In Jesus' reasoning, our ability to keep praying equals having faith in Him.

A lifestyle of regular prayer is evidence of faith. In other words, the converse is also true: prayerlessness is a clear indication of not having or being in the faith. What if Jesus comes and finds me unworthy of Him because I refused to pray consistently? I could be rejected not because I refused to go to church or be kind or be the employee of the month or best mom, but because I refused to pray. That is some scary stuff to me!

The bottom line is it is impossible to love an invisible God (He doesn't even want us to make images depicting Him) without talking to, calling upon, and praying to Him. Just as one can't have an earthly relationship, be it marriage or friendship or work arrangement, without some basic form of communication and awareness of the existence of the other party. Thus, prayer is fundamental to the life of the Believer, if indeed, we truly are His.

> [9] And they sung a new song, saying, "Thou art worthy to take the book, and to open the seals thereof: for thou wast slain, and hast redeemed us to God by thy blood out of every kindred, and tongue, and people, and nation";[10] *And hast made us unto our God kings and priests: and we shall reign on the earth.* (Rev. 5:10, KJV).

Now while it could be possible to have some special earthly arrangement (typically dysfunctional) that may allow, for example, a boss and employee to never see each other and still have some rudimentary forms of communication, Our God is not a God of dysfunction and this is not how He wants to engage with us.

He is the God of Love who uses several metaphors to illustrate His feelings for us: we are His bride. We are engraved (tattooed) in the palms of His hands. We are the apple of His eye. He has loved us with an everlasting love. He is married to the backslider and countless others.

If you aren't proud of your prayer life, please don't let guilt and condemnation leave you bound and in a continued strained relationship with God. This would be the enemy's greatest desire because you are a threat to the kingdom of darkness when you pray effectively.

Until we recognize and truthfully acknowledge our weaknesses and failings, we are never going to make any effort to fix them. And the good news is, it's not up to us to fix ourselves by ourselves. As children of God, He gives us all the tools we need to address every deficiency in our lives with the help of the Holy Spirit.

## THOUGHTS AND TIPS ON PRAYER EXECUTION:

1. The parable in Luke 18: 1-8 speaks about the woman praying daily for a long time, asking God to settle her case. The over-arching goal Jesus seems to be pointing to is consistency as well as persistence, both critical tools for our success

in answered prayer. How do you plan on building both your consistency and persistence?
2. I admit that many times, prayer feels burdensome to me. It can be intense work. How do you overcome those times when your flesh doesn't want to comply with what God demands of you?

## Prayer Points

- ❖ Father, give me grace to seek your mind and Word out for my specific situations I am facing.
- ❖ Holy Spirit, you are the revelator. Take the Word of God and blow it up to me I pray in Jesus' name. Come and walk alongside me and show me the secrets I need to know in your Word.
- ❖ I pray in Jesus' name that the grace to accept and obey your revealed Word will come up on me.
- ❖ In the mighty name of Jesus, I repel every evil bird that would dare to steal the good seed that you deposit in my heart., even as the parable of the sower explains.
- ❖ Father, let the conditions in my heart be right and ripe for your Word to bear forth great fruits of success, power, answered prayer and righteousness in my life. Anything that would be hostile to your Word, I command it to die in the mighty name of Jesus.
- ❖ Holy Spirit, build consistency and persistence in me. Your word says that if I faint in the day of adversity then my faith is small. Give me staying power, I pray, in the mighty name of Jesus.

# CHAPTER 3

# THE PERILS OF PRAYERLESSNESS

*"If the Christian does not allow prayer to drive sin out of his life, sin will drive prayer out of his life. Like light and darkness, the two cannot dwell together." – M.E. Andross*

*Gracious and ever merciful Lord, please forgive me for my negligence in praying. Remove me far from the land of spiritual complacency and slumber and with your Holy Spirit's help, plant me firmly as a watchman of prayer in your army. In Jesus' name I pray, Amen.*

## ORIGINAL SIN

Sin is more than a set of activities that are displeasing to God. Sin is a condition, a state of being or existence in which we are separated from God. This condition is a perversion of what God originally designed us to be, and wills for us as His beloved children.

I am dedicating this section here to sin because we are dangerously deceived when we narrow our understanding or definition of sin to fit into a neatly packaged box of things we can or can't do, like a set of rules posted on the wall of a swimming pool. We conveniently make it a tidy checklist of the Ten Commandments and we smugly believe in our hearts that since we didn't *actively* trespass in those areas, (or asked for forgiveness) we are ok and there is nothing else to pray about. Such is the overwhelming deception and pervasiveness of sin.

Sin is inherent to the current human condition, thanks to the Fall. In theory, when we become born again, our spirits are reborn, regenerated, and re-connected with God through Christ. That vital link to God must always be nurtured to bring and sustain spiritual growth. The Word of God and praying are the two major ways by which our spiritual growth happens. Our old sinful nature (which is comprised of desires, tendencies, attitudes, thoughts, habits, mindsets, and behaviors) has to be continually brought to heel. Our sinful nature must be and submerged under the control of our renewed spirits and directed by God through prayer and His Word. When we don't pray, our old man (or sinful nature) rises and starts to smother the renewed spiritual life in us.

## A False Sense of Security

There is a strong correlation between comfort and ease, and the penchant for ignoring or refusing to serve God. This is very true in developed nations which are mostly post-Christian, and at the micro level, in our individual hearts. We tend to ignore God when things are going great, or at least, decently enough and then only start calling out to Him when we are in a tight spot, which is exactly what I did.

When I look back at my earlier Christian life and my failure to engage in a consistent prayer lifestyle, I feel that some of my difficulties and underlying issues contributing to them could have been avoided, or mitigated, if I had been obedient in praying. This is especially evident when I compared myself to the friends who did have a consistent prayer life. Their lives tended to be steadier and smoother. The gap widens even more when I look at those who came from actively serving born-again families. The latter reaped the harvest of generational prayers sown even before their birth. What a blessing that is!

## LIABILITIES AND RISKS

Just as there are advantages and blessings that come with obedience, there are also liabilities and risks we expose ourselves to when we don't pray, or have an anemic prayer life. The Bible bears me out on this. Job 21:7-21 is an interesting passage that illustrates the very real dangers of prayerlessness, especially for protracted periods. In it, Job starts by complaining about the wicked man's life of luxury and enjoyment: his home is in a safe community, his livestock (in our day income and investments) increase on cue. The wicked man and his family enjoy life, dance, and they spend their days in wealth. With trouble seemingly so far away, the wicked then start to question their need for God:

> Therefore, they say unto God, *Depart from us; for we desire not the knowledge of thy ways. What is the Almighty, that we should serve him? And what profit should we have, if we pray unto him?* Lo, their good is not in their hand: the counsel of the wicked is far from me. How oft is the candle of the wicked put out! and how oft cometh their destruction upon them! God distributeth sorrows in his anger.[18] They are as stubble before the wind, and as chaff that the storm carrieth away. God layeth up his iniquity for his children: he rewardeth him, and he shall know it. His eyes shall see his destruction, and he shall drink of the wrath of the Almighty. (Job 21:14-21, KJV).

Prayerlessness first manifests itself as a lack of desire to know God's ways. It could come from complacency or a failure to nurture a vibrant relationship with the Lord. We may not outright tell God to leave us alone, but our inactions and or disobedience say just as much when we don't pray. Slowly we relegate Him to the outskirts of our lives, quench the Holy Spirit, and possibly even force Him to leave us. This is what happened in King Saul's life.

At the root of prayerlessness is a lack of appreciation for God and everything He stands for. Then, we take who He is for granted. The need to be in vital connection with Him becomes less and less of a priority. In our eyes, we make Him too small or our equal. We gain a false sense of security because our comfortable lives create an illusion of self-sufficiency. Self-sufficiency is one of the Believer's greatest enemies. We either depend on God or we depend on something else. That something else could be anything, including rationalization. Depending on anyone or anything other than God (including ourselves) is a sin because we make that thing a god, or idol. The very first commandment is "Thou shall have no other gods before me." (Exod. 20:3, KJV).

This illusion of self-sufficiency, thanks to our economic status, is described by Jesus as the "deceitfulness of riches" and he references it in the parable of the sower as one of the reasons why Christians fall away:

> He also that received seed among the thorns is he that heareth the word; and the care of this world, and the *deceitfulness of riches, choke the word, and he becometh unfruitful.* (Matt. 13:22, KJV).

Going back to Job's passage, our comfortable lives can cause us to fail to see how we benefit from prayer because we are in a predictable, protected, and prosperous situation. When we don't see how we profit from prayer, we don't pray. But while this world is busy rocking us to spiritual slumber, we don't realize we are losing control of our own spiritual health and well-being. Our candle (believed to mean life, favor, prosperity) can be easily put out. We become easy targets for destruction, hence the often-repeated scripture 1 Peter 5:8 in which we are told to "Be sober, be vigilant, because your adversary the Devil, as a roaring lion, walketh about, seeking who he may devour." Prayerlessness, therefore makes us easily identifiable in the spirit realm for spiritual attacks. It leaves us vulnerable and unpredicted.

Spiritual attacks typically manifest themselves in the natural as turbulent, potentially life-altering events. These events may not necessarily as intense as Job's ordeals, but are just as painful and puzzling. Our lack of vigilance in prayer erodes our once-solid foundation. We are more susceptible to being blown away by tempestuous situations. The Bible tells us that tempestuous storms come to everyone but the differentiator is that the ones who practice what is expected of them (pray) are able to control the outcome of their situation. Their good then is in their own hands.

> Therefore, whosoever heareth these sayings of mine, and doeth them, I will liken him unto a wise man, which built his house upon a rock: And the rain descended, and the floods came, and the winds blew, and beat upon that house; and it fell not: for it was founded upon a rock. *And every one that heareth these sayings of mine, and doeth them not, shall be likened unto a foolish man, which built his house upon the sand: And the rain descended, and the floods came, and the winds blew, and beat upon that house; and it fell: and great was the fall of it.* (Matt. 7:24-27, KJV).

R.A. Torrey, a great revivalist and man of prayer says, "The reason why many fail in battle is because they wait until the hour of battle. The reason why others succeed is because they have gained their victory on their knees long before the battle came... Anticipate your battles; fight them on your knees before temptation comes and you will always have the victory."

Isaiah 56 is an interesting chapter because it shares both the benefits of serving God faithfully (which by default includes praying), and the perils of prayerlessness. In the first six verses, the Lord promises there are rewards for those who have joined themselves to (or married) the Lord, choose the things that please Him and those who keep His covenant:

> Even them will I bring to my holy mountain, and make them joyful in my house of prayer: their burnt offerings and their sacrifices shall be accepted upon mine altar;

for mine house shall be called an house of prayer for all people. (Isaiah 56:7, KJV).

Those rewards include (1) going to a more elevated place of prayer, (2) being made joyful because prayers are being answered, and (3) offerings and sacrifices being acceptable to God.

## KING SAUL: A CAUTIONARY TALE

The flip side is frightening pronouncement for God's watchmen, who are supposed to be keeping guard spiritually but have been rocked to spiritual slumber. We are not invited to that even greater place of prayer. Instead, wicked beasts from the fields and the forests are released to torment and devour us:

> All ye beasts of the field, come to devour, yea, all ye beasts in the forest. His watchmen are blind: they are all ignorant, they are all dumb dogs, they cannot bark; sleeping, lying down, *loving to slumber*. Yea, they are *greedy dogs which can never have enough*, and they are shepherds that cannot understand: *they all look to their own way, everyone for his gain, from his quarter*. (Isaiah 56:9-11, KJV).

In this passage, "beasts" are representative of evil spirits or demons unleashed on the people of God who have backslidden and aren't praying. King Saul was the poster boy of this kind of backsliding because, after stubbornly disobeying the Lord and refusing to amend his ways he eventually succumbed to terrible inter-generational destruction. Destruction took over Saul's whole household. Saul, his three sons, and his grandchildren were all wiped out in one day.

A closer look at King Saul's life shows how he walked away from a strong relationship with God: it was to his ultimate detriment and demise. Saul was once a man greatly favored and loved by God. He was chosen to be the first king of Israel and the Lord moved mightily in his life, even filling him with the Holy Spirit so that he prophesied with a company of prophets, something that was such a highly unusual occurrence for someone who wasn't a priest or prophet that it even prompted a saying among the people of Israel.

But over time, as Saul clung to power at all costs, disobeyed God's instructions, and worried more about how he looked in the eyes of men, the Spirit of God lifted from him. The spirit of God was replaced by an evil spirit that tormented Saul. He had once enjoyed the presence of the Holy Spirit but now in the absence of the Holy Spirit and counsel from the prophets, he feverishly searched for guidance from a witch as seen in 1 Samuel 28:1-20. Saul's backslidden state eventually cost him everything: the kingship was ripped from his possession and his whole family was killed in such a way that there would never be a descendant of his to contend for the throne.

## Watchman and Watch Dogs

God's people are supposed to be His watchmen. Watchmen are trained warriors who stay at their posts watchfully guarding their lives, families and communities, while watching and waiting for the arrival of our bridegroom, Jesus, not unlike the ten virgins in Matthew 25. We are supposed to be watchmen instead of dumb watch dogs. Watch dogs are supposed to sit alert with their ears cocked and eyes peeled. But when we become dumb watch dogs, we unable to remain alert, fall sleep or eat the treats the enemy offers and let him through without any resistance. This is what we are like when we don't pray. We lack true revelation and understanding, and miss impending dangers.

Furthermore, prayerlessness causes us to become indifferent, weak, mute and, unable to address or confront things we are meant to deal with in prayer. 1 Samuel 2:12-4:22 tells the pitiful story of Eli. Eli was once a powerful prophet, but over time, Eli weakened and became an indulgent father who allowed his two sons to commit many atrocities while serving under him as priests. Eli's sons even slept with women who came to the temple to worship God (does this sound familiar?) Eli and his sons' rejection of God's ways came at a very steep price. The Bible says that the Word (revelation) of the Lord became very scarce. There were no open visions in the land. Eli himself lost his eyesight due to his advanced age, but it was a symptom and representation of the spiritual condition of the country as a whole. While he and his family were slipping further into depravation, Samuel, was growing in favor with God, seeking Him and being instructed in the service of the Lord.

The Lord appeared to Samuel with specific news about His plans to punish Eli's family and Israel, for their falling away. Eli's family was going to be destroyed in battle, and God cursed them that no man in Eli's household would ever live to a good old age. This was astoundingly horrible news that you wouldn't wish on your worst enemy. But, as if this pronouncement wasn't bad enough, when Eli was informed of God's plan, his tepid, indifferent response was simply dumb-founding: "It is the Lord: let him do what seemeth him good." (1 Sam.3:18, KJV).

Eli's tolerance of sin and prayerlessness in the younger generation had made him a blind dog. It had also muted him and weakened him to the point where he couldn't resist the evil that was coming his family's way, or stand in the gap by interceding for them. Eli was essentially a dumb watch dog who couldn't bark, lulled by sleep and a lack of watchfulness.

For a quick comparison, between Eli and Abram, we see that Abram was much more alert spiritually and prepared to stand in the gap for his nephew, Lot when he was going astray. After Lot chose to live in and associate with the wicked culture of Sodom, *twice*, Abram intervened on Lot's behalf and spared him from great destruction. The first time, Abram and his army waged war and physically retrieved Lot from his captors after he and his family were kidnapped as prisoners of war in Genesis chapter 14 and then in Genesis chapter 18, when he negotiated with God for Sodom and Gomorrah to be spared for the sake of his nephew Lot. In both situations, Abram got the desire of his heart and his nephew and family were spared.

We can choose to be Abram or we can choose to be Eli. Either alternative is firmly within the realm of possibility and totally our choice to make. We can rise up and with God's help push back the agenda of wickedness before it fully manifests and wreaks havoc, or we can be passive and get steam-rolled by our wicked enemy.

## SELF-CENTERED, SELF-INDULGENT, AND NEVER SATISFIED

Based on Isaiah 56:9-11, another peril of prayerlessness is that it makes us become self-centered *(they all look to their own way, everyone for his gain, from his quarter)*, self-indulgent *(loving to slumber)*, and never satisfied *(greedy dogs which can never have enough)*. Instead of having a heart for the unsaved and the world that Christ wants us to win to enlarge His territory, we become only interested in whatever directly concerns us alone and not the Master. We are more resistant to denying ourselves in fasting or giving up anything for the sake of the greater things God purposes. Additionally, we are never satisfied and keep wanting more, coveting with others have as well. Paul cautioned against this when he reminded Timothy that "godliness with contentment is great gain" (1 Tim. 6:6).

None of these qualities are fit for the Master's use. He doesn't take us higher to His holy mountain where we experience all kinds of rewards (referenced in Isaiah 56:7-8). In the case of the foolish virgins, they are locked out of the bridegroom's presence. He refuses to let them in after the doors are locked, saying: "I know you not, Watch therefore, for ye know neither the day nor the hour wherein the Son of man cometh." (Matt. 25:12-13, KJV). In this parable, the virgins run out of oil (the Holy Spirit) for their lamps (the Word) and they are forced to leave their posts to go find more oil because the bridegroom delays and the night stretches much longer than they anticipated. In their absence, Jesus the bridegroom arrives and denies them access to the party (the kingdom) because they were unprepared and unavailable. They are ultimately unable to make it into great feast when the bridegroom and His bride the church are united.

My heart aches from seeing and hearing so many stories of wrecked Christian marriages, horrible sicknesses, wayward Christian children, and backslidden parents. It's true no one is exempt from difficulties, but so many of our responses to and outcomes of our problems are just not showing the glory or power of God. In fact, these situations reflect poorly on our so-called All-Mighty God. They reveal our weakened state which can attract and perpetuate

Satanic strongholds down the family blood line (generational curses) as we saw in Eli's family's case where God told them that no male would live a long full life. Consequently, we have lots of defeated and bewildered Christians going through all kinds of issues but incapable of recognizing the spiritual reasons behind them because we are not actively seeking the Lord for the answers to the underlying problems and the power to tackle them.

Unfortunately, even to this day, there are many families that for whatever reason are stalked by curses like premature death, chronic poverty, rage, suicide, promiscuity, and many others. Sadly, there are many ill-advised Christians operating under the assumption that simply because they have given their lives to Christ, they are immune from any such generational liabilities all while these issues routinely crop up and decimate lives, all while they look on and helplessly shrug their shoulders, while many churches are complicit by either not teaching the truth on these issues and/or lack the skills needed to break these bondages.

Thankfully, the concept of deliverance as a ministry within the body of Christ is now seeing a resurgence. There are many ministries that teach self-deliverance and a few that also specialize in doing deliverance for those who request such services.

## THE FULL IMPLICATION

It is my prayer that as we understand the full implications of not having a regular prayer life and how high the stakes are. This chapter isn't meant to scare anyone. It is meant to show how kind our Father actually is, and how serious life is because we still have an enemy who wants to exact legally sanctioned judgment and trouble on the people of God. Yes, we serve a God of love and yes, we have grace abounding toward us, but we also have a <u>real enemy</u> who is looking for people to devour. He actively petitions for people's lives to be destroyed as we see he did in both Job chapter 1 and Zechariah 3:1-4, where he stood against Joshua to accuse him before God. Giving him a toe-hold in our lives by disobeying God or neglecting our spiritual duties potentially opens us up for real trouble. Our merciful Father often times seems very harsh and punitive but it's because as our just Protector, He cannot shield us ad infinitum when we deliberately leave the door open for evil to come into our lives. Legally, the enemy can petition and be given permission to oppress even Christians, especially when we are negligent of God's commands.

In chapter 9, Enter the Dragon, we will deal more with the topic of our adversary. For now, I want you to understand that Satan is the Accuser of the Brethren and actively petitions God to bring evil our way. If he does this for righteous law-abiding people like Joshua the high priest and Job a man who routinely stood in the gap for his family and offered sacrifices on their behalf, then we can only imagine what the average Christian could potentially be up against. This is why Jesus, in teaching the disciples to pray advised them to pray to be delivered from evil.

When we don't pray and no prayer seeds are deposited on our behalf, we are more likely to fall prey to the enemy's desire to devour us. Prayer is a vitally needed covering that deliberately and pro-actively counteracts, neutralizes or minimizes the schemes and activities of the powers of darkness.

Eli could have turned away from his wicked ways on behalf of his children but chose not to. Likewise, God gave Saul a long period of time to repent—just ask David who had to endure several grueling years on the run from him. But Saul and Eli chose to ignore the grace of God and continue in their passive or active participation in sin. They could have been spared, even as Lot was spared because of Abraham's righteousness and prayer life. But, they didn't bother to draw near to God again.

Dear Friend, may this never be your story, in Jesus' name. Don't allow yourself to stay disconnected from the Lord or weak in your prayer life. He has great rewards and victories for you if you will seek God while He may be found. Let us seek Him together. Let us work together to get you back on track. Please check out the resources on www.prayslayandreign.com that are available for you to take advantage of, including private prayer consultations. Be committed to making this transformation happen. Let's go from pitiful to powerful, in Jesus' name. AMEN.

## THOUGHTS AND TIPS ON PRAYER EXECUTION

1. In what ways are self-centeredness, self-indulgence and a lack of satisfaction evident in our present world? How are these things eroding your walk with the Lord?
2. How do I keep the oil (Holy Spirit) in my lamp from running out? What areas of sin may I be consciously or unconsciously allowing the enemy to use against me in accusation?

## PRAYER POINTS

- ❖ Father, forgive me for the sin of prayerlessness, I pray in the mighty name of Jesus.
- ❖ Any evil beasts that have been dispatched to attack my life or my family, as a result of my weak prayer life, let the blood of Jesus repel them even now I pray.
- ❖ Holy Spirit, give me a way of escape out of prayerlessness, I pray.
- ❖ Abba, in the name of Jesus, increase my dependence on you I pray. I pray for less of me, Lord, and more of you, Lord.
- ❖ Let the lines of communication between me and my Father be opened up in the mighty name of Jesus Christ.
- ❖ Holy Spirit, connect me back to the Father I pray. Breathe life into my prayer life I pray.
- ❖ Show me how to come back to you and deepen my commitment to a stronger prayer life.

CHAPTER 4

# God's Purpose for Creating Man

*Prayer lays hold of God's plan and becomes the link between His will and its accomplishment on earth. Amazing things happen, and we are given the privilege of being the channels of the Holy Spirit's prayer. – Elisabeth Elliot*

*Dear Lord, I know you had a specific plan for me when you created me. Reveal to me the specifics of my destiny and I pray that through this journey of Praying, Slaying, and Reigning, you will set my feet on a collision course with the fulfillment of everything you created me to accomplish on this earth. Thank you in advance for what You have to teach me now. Amen.*

## Man's Purpose – Why we were created

Before we can successfully understand the tools critical for prevailing prayer, we first need to understand what the purpose of man is and why we were created. There is a lot to unpack here so please pray for your spiritual eyes to be opened to enable understanding to be able to grasp everything.

When we examine the book of Genesis, we realize that God, who is a spirit being (John 4:24), the Ultimate Ruler and King of all Kings (1 Tim. 6:15) created the earth and everything in it with the specific intent that mankind and mankind alone was supposed to rule or have dominion over everything in this earth realm.

> Then God said, "Let us make mankind in our image, in our likeness, *so that they* may rule over the fish in the sea and the birds in the sky, over the livestock and all the wild animals, and over all the creatures that move along the ground." (Gen. 1:26, NIV).

It is important to note that the ability to rule flows as a natural extension of who God is and who He created us to be. Kingship is inherent in God. He is the Eternal King (1 Tim. 1:7) and so man, created in His likeness is also expected to rule. It was part of our divine heritage, prior to the fall and still remains our heritage after Jesus' restoration of our lost privileges:

> [5] And from Jesus Christ, who is the faithful witness, and the first-begotten of the dead, and the prince of the kings of the earth. Unto him that loved us, and washed us from our sins in his own blood, [6] *And hath made us kings and priests unto God and his Father*; to him be glory and dominion for ever and ever. Amen. (Rev. 1:5-6, KJV).

Jesus has made us kings and priests for God our Father. Following this line of reasoning, God, the Possessor of the Heavens and the earth (Genesis 14:19) has His own domain or territory He rules over and He created humans in His image and gave mankind his own territory (Earth) to rule over. The earth was in a sense, leased over to Adam to occupy till the landlord (God) returns and takes back His rule over it. God placed man (Adam) in the Garden of Eden to work it and take care of it (Genesis 2:15).

The New Testament bears out this theory as well. The imagery carries over to Jesus' teaching. In the Parable of the Tenants (Mark 12:1-9), a ruler or noble man leases his property, a vineyard, while he goes away for a trip. A lease does not imply ownership of a property, but a responsibility to care for and tend it. The owner will eventually come back and re-claim it. Likewise, we have been given a lease to take total care of the earth in every dimension—physical and spiritual.

The only authorized beings on Earth, are the birds of the air, the fish of the sea, the animals on the earth and finally the crown jewel of God's creation, man. No one, not even God, who is a Spirit, and is the Owner of the earth is lawfully permitted to stay on Earth because God is a spirit and in order to live on the earth, you need a physical body made from the earth. Here is a shocking truth, and the importance of its revelation is not to be taken lightly: God's plan for this dispensation of time was for *Adam* (us) to be in control of and in charge of the earth. The earth is man's jurisdiction to oversee and enforce God's way of doing things in it until the lease expires:

> The heaven, even the heavens, are the LORD's: but the earth hath he given to the children of men. (Psalm 115:16, KJV).

It is therefore fallacious to say things like "God is in control of the earth" because it is simply NOT TRUE. God can't be in control because He doesn't have a physical body. He is a spirit being which is why He needed Adam on the earth in the first place. Adam was in control of the earth and he inadvertently handed it over to Satan. The control or rule of the earth is now firmly in Satan's grip. God, being faithful to His own Word and contract, will never go against His own Word, even if there has been some corruption in the original agreement.

Just as the Canadian Prime Minister cannot come to the United States of America and appoint a new Supreme Court justice, God cannot and will not come to Earth and take Adam's (mankind's) mandated role away from him until the lease expires. To do so would render God unfaithful, untruthful, and untrustworthy. Therefore, when people blame God for bad things happening, their reasoning is fundamentally flawed and based on incomplete knowledge. When people get upset with God for "allowing" evil to over-run their circumstances, their disappointment and or anger toward God is completely misplaced. *We* abandoned our responsibilities and have given evil the upper hand in the affairs of men. The logical antidote is to rise up, take our rightful place as kings and priests and pray, partnering with God to undo and prevent (subdue) the enemy's activities.

We humans, children of Adam, are an interesting hybrid. We are in fact made up of three distinct parts: spirit, soul, and body.

> May God himself, the God of peace, sanctify you through and through. *May your whole spirit, soul, and body* be kept blameless at the coming of our Lord Jesus Christ. (1 Thess. 5:25, KJV).

You may have heard it preached that we humans are spirits, who live in bodies and have souls. You are not your body. You are not your soul. You are a spirit being, like your Heavenly Father. You just happen to be having a transient earthly experience. We also know this because the Bible teaches us that God (a spirit being) first created Adam as a spirit being:

> So, God created man in his own image, in the image of God created he him; male and female created he them. Genesis 1:27 (KJV).

Spirits never die. They are eternal. Just as God is immortal, so are we. We humans are eternal and we will continue to live even after we leave our physical bodies on this planet. The question has never been if we live forever, but where? We are the ones who individually choose where we get to spend eternity: with God in Heaven or in Hell which was designed for Satan and his rebellious angels.

In the following chapter of Genesis, God created a physical body out of the dirt for Adam to live in and navigate the earth with. Then

God breathed into Adam's nostrils, at which point man became a living soul.

> And the LORD God *formed man of the dust of the ground*, and breathed into his nostrils the breath of life; and man became a *living soul*. (Genesis 2:7, KJV).

It's easy to miss this distinction, perhaps even assume that the Bible was being repetitive but actually, there were two different times (quoted above) in which God is recorded being at work in putting Adam together. The first time, He *created* Adam as a spirit, made in God's image. The second time, God *formed* Adam out of the dust; in other words, He made a physical body for him. Finally, with the breathing of God's breath into the clay body is when the *soulish* part of Adam came into existence. The soul is the intermediary between the spirit man and flesh. It is made up of the intellect, will, emotions, and conscience. The soul is mortal and does perish and is distinctly different from the spirit. Hence, many theologians teach this: "I am not my soul. I am a spirit first. I live in a body and I have a soul."

The tripartite nature of man is important, especially in the light of prevailing prayer because, with our salvation, our once-dead spirits are reborn or made alive (hence the expression we become "born again"). We are now able to communicate with God as we were originally intended to. Mankind's fellowship with God is restored at the born-again experience and must be renewed and maintained by feeding the spirit man and staying in connection with the Spirit of God, the Holy Spirit.

## GOD'S INSTRUCTIONS TO ADAM

Upon the creation of man, God gave instructions to Adam outlining his responsibilities (a job description!) as a tenant leasing property from his landlord.

> God blessed them and said to them, *"Be fruitful and increase in number; fill the earth and <u>subdue</u> it. Rule over the fish in the sea and the birds in the sky and over every living creature that moves on the ground."* (Gen. 1:28, NIV).

God instructed His creation to "be fruitful and increase." I believe that God's instruction was both for physical as well as spiritual reproduction: the born-again Christian has a mandate to bring more lives into the Kingdom of God (Mark 16:15).

God placed Adam in a beautiful and decked out garden - planted by God Himself! Adam was then put in charge of beautifying and maintaining the garden: And the LORD God took the man, and put him into the garden of Eden to dress it and to keep it (Gen. 2:15, KJV). Adam and Eve had the whole garden to tend. They were also told what not to do and warned that disobedience would mean death. The only thing they couldn't do was eat of the fruit of the tree of the knowledge of good and evil (Gen. 2:17).

> The woman said to the serpent, "We may eat fruit from the trees in the garden, ³ but God did say, 'You *must not eat fruit from the tree* that is in the middle of the garden, and you must not touch it, *or you will die.*'" (Gen. 3:2-3, NIV).

Everything was going great until Eve disobeyed God, Adam came along for the ride and they were kicked out of the Garden to go fend for themselves (Genesis 3:23). They failed to perform their job satisfactorily (or fulfill the terms of their lease's contract) and as such, were given the pink slip and evicted out of the garden.

## CREATED FOR GOD'S PLEASURE

God made us to please Him, to bring Him pleasure. According to Revelations 4:11b. all things, including people, were created for God's pleasure:

> "Thou art worthy, O Lord, to receive glory and honor and power: for thou hast created all things, and for thy pleasure they are and were created." (KJV).

He genuinely loves to hear from us, communicate and work with us. This is something He greatly derives pleasure from as evidenced by the fact that God relished Adam and Eve's company and worked collaboratively with them:

> "And out of the ground, the LORD God formed every beast of the field, and every fowl of the air; and brought them unto Adam to see what he would call them: and whatsoever Adam called every living creature, that was the name thereof. And Adam gave names to all cattle, and to the fowl of the air, and to every beast of the field;" (Gen. 2:19-20a, KJV).

We were created to have communion and work with Him, with the Lord lovingly checking in on us and getting updates over the course of the execution of the assigned work. God would come to the Garden to literally "hang out" with Adam and Eve until their sin cut them off and suddenly made them incapable of being in His presence anymore:

> "And they heard the voice of the LORD God walking in the garden in the cool of the day: and Adam and his wife hid themselves from the presence of the LORD God amongst the trees of the garden." (Gen. 3:8, KJV).

## SPIRITUAL DEATH

The significance of the consequences of their disobedience cannot be overstated or ignored. Just as they had been warned, Adam and Eve died *spiritually*. Ezekiel 18:20a (KJV) says, "The soul that sinneth, it shall die" Because of their disobedience, they lost most of their spiritual abilities: living, seeing, walking and communicating with God on a continuous basis. Prior to the fall, they were able to talk to and go for walks with God who is a spirit, when He would come visit "in the cool of the day" (Genesis 3:8).

Spiritual death meant that men would now be controlled by their flesh and soul (the carnal nature). Men could no longer operate as a spirit being with the power to rule both the spiritual and physical dimensions of the earth. Since nature hates a vacuum, the loss of spiritual power meant the stark reality and consequences of handing over their dominion, or right to rule the earth, to Satan the Deceiver.

The other part of this wretched fall is that since they hadn't yet procreated, we (their descendants) also fell. Because of Adam, we inherited original sin (Romans 5:12) from birth (Psalm 51:5). In this we humans are all equal: "for all have sinned and fall short of the glory of God," (Romans 3:23, NIV). Our collective birthright as royalty and rulers was intercepted by the Deceiver, Satan.

## SATAN: "THE GOD OF THIS WORLD"

How do we know that man handed over his authority as ruler to the Devil? Because we know that when Jesus was being tempted by Satan, Jesus was promised all power if He would bow down and worship him:

> Then Jesus was led by the Spirit into the wilderness to be tempted by the Devil. Again, the Devil took him to a very high mountain and showed him all the kingdoms of the world and their splendor. "All this I will give you," he said, "if you will bow down and worship me." [10] Jesus said to him, "Away from me, Satan! For it is written: 'Worship the Lord your God, and serve him only.'" (Matthew 4:1, 8-10, NIV).

Jesus never disputed Satan's ownership of the world in this confrontation because He knew Satan was correct. In fact, Jesus referred to Satan at other times as the "prince of this world" (John 14:30). In 2 Corinthians 4:4, Satan is called "the god of this world." We will examine more things about the Devil in chapter 8.

Since man, the crown jewel of God's creation, is the only authorized being on Earth with a free will, we are the only ones who can accomplish meaningful things here on Earth. No one, not even God, who is a Spirit, and is the Owner of the earth is lawfully permitted to stay on Earth because God is a spirit and in order to live on the earth, you need a physical body made from the earth. This is why it is impossible for God to fully be in control on Earth. He only has his foot soldiers, humans who will yield to Him. We will read later how God used the Son of Man, Jesus to stay within the confines of this rule and still defeated the enemy to retrieve our rulership back to man.

Likewise, Satan is a spirit and has no earthly body either. So, by definition, he can't be here on Earth for long either. He consequently primarily uses men, worldly systems including entertainment, social constructs like economic classes and traditions of men, worldly kingdoms, and demons (fallen angels) to propagate all kinds of wickedness, darkness, bondage, and sickness in the earth. Satan is the king of this world (2 Corinthians 4:4) and he rules it wickedly. The battle between good and evil, both in the heavenlies and on earth, is essentially a tug of war for the souls of men to advance each camp's kingdom.

Because the earth is still for the children of men, even God, when He needed to come to Earth to rectify the fall and mend the break between Himself and Adam, had to use a human being. That human being was Jesus Christ, the immaculately conceived son of Mary. Jesus was fully God and fully human (John 1:1-5, John 1:14, Hebrews 2:14). In the fullness of time, God sent His son, Jesus so He could properly represent God on Earth, carry out God's work on Earth and show men how to do the same (John 3:16).

## THE PLAN BEFORE THE FALL

Thankfully, our all-knowing and only wise God had prepared a contingency plan ahead of the fall to ensure that humanity wasn't left stranded with no escape route. Jesus is that escape route. We learn that we were redeemed by the precious blood of Jesus ...

> "[20] Who verily was foreordained before the foundation of the world, but was manifest in these last times for you who by him do believe in God that He raised him up from the dead, and gave him glory, that your faith and hope might be in God." (1 Peter 1:20-21, KJV).

Jesus was already there before the creation of the world. Here is a second passage that further elaborates the truth of this:

> **1** In the beginning was the Word, and the Word was with God, and the Word was God. **²** He was with God in the beginning. **³** Through him all things were made; without him nothing was made that has been made. (John 1:1-3, NIV).

God foretold in Genesis (when He was speaking to the serpent):

> And I will put enmity between you and the woman, and between your offspring and hers; he will crush your head, and you will strike his heel." (Gen. 3:15, NIV).

We see Jesus fulfilling this promise by destroying the very government of Satan in His death, resurrection, and elevation to the right hand of God: "For this purpose, the Son of God was manifested, that he might destroy the works of the Devil." (1 John 3:8b, KJV). It is now our job to emulate Jesus and continue His mandate that He started in the earth and we will discuss Jesus in greater detail under the revelation of Jesus Christ.

## In Summary We Were Created to:

1. Rule and have dominion over the earth. (Genesis 1:28, 2:19-20a).
2. Multiply and enlarge our spiritual and natural presence as God's representatives on the earth. (Genesis 1:28, 2:19-20a).
3. Beautify, or dress, and maintain the earth, while subduing unruly elements (Genesis 2:15).
4. Work collaboratively with God (Genesis 1:27, 2:18, 21-25).
5. Have communion with God. (Psalm 16:7).
6. Emulate Christ and continue His work (1 Corinthians 11:1).

## Our Purpose and Prevailing Prayer

Now that we know what God's original purpose for creating man is, and the parameters surrounding that creation, what that does have to do with prevailing prayer? Everything. God can do nothing on Earth great or small without the willful cooperation of human beings. This is because this is order in which He set things up and Earth is NOT His domain to fully rule just yet and Adam's lease for managing the earth is currently in Satan's hands.

God will not and does not override the free will of the people He created. Unlike the Devil, God doesn't force or drive anyone against their will. We have to *choose* to be used by Him, in matters great and small, all day and every day and to "use your body as an instrument to do what is right for the glory of God" (Romans 6:13b, NLT). We must humble ourselves and offer ourselves as living sacrifices (Romans 12:1). God has no hands, voice or feet on Earth, except for the earthly bodies that allow themselves to be used by Him.

We established previously that **prevailing prayer** is prayer that overcomes natural and supernatural circumstances by super-imposing or enforcing God's will over the natural order or progression of the world. It is operative. Prevailing prayer changes people, situations, and things (both natural and spiritual) by enforcing God's mind, Word and Will to manifest in the earth realm. The Believer who chooses to align themselves with God in prayer is in a sense like a law enforcement officer. They utilize God's delegated power and authority to allow or disallow things from happening or to dress and maintain the earth. Prevailing prayer, therefore, is productive and brings results. In other words, *it is effective* or effectual. James 5:16b explains that "the effectual, fervent prayer of a righteous man availeth (or accomplishes) much." Effective prayer allows man to unify with God in a way that allows His purposes and plans to be established and executed on Earth to expand and multiply His Kingdom, as we were created to do. This is why prevailing prayer is so vitally important.

When Christians have a lax attitude toward prayer, assuming that "What will be, will be" and "God is in control regardless of what I do", we are refusing to partner with God. We limit His abilities to effect change in the earth realm. We miss what we were designed to so and fail in our job description, which calls for us to subdue, maintain, and beautify the earth by working the works of God. These are the same instructions He gave to Adam (Genesis 1:26, 1:28, 2:19-20a, 2:15; Psalm 115:16). We are also missing out on the blessing of making ourselves available for God's pleasure, which is what we were created to do (Revelations 4:11). There are grave consequences to prayerlessness but unfortunately, we rarely hear about them. The lack of knowledge of these consequences do not negate their existence or exempt us from experiencing them. In fact, many of the problems we are individually and corporately facing in the body of Christ are directly tied to our prayerlessness as covered in Chapter 2, The Perils of Prayerlessness.

Prayer then gives God permission to move on Earth. As John Wesley (1703-1791) put it "God does nothing except in response to believing prayer." As I have learned more about my originally intended purpose for being on this earth, the Lord has shown me how to exercise my spiritual birthrights and increase my dominion in the earth through prayer. I have also seen many people rise up in this same way.

Activities of the enemy are to be subdued and brought under my control, as God intended when He created Adam and Eve. One example of this came from a lesson I learned from my prayer coach who taught me how to command my morning like the king that I was created to be. It is a prayer based on the Scripture Job 38:12 (NIV):

> "Have you ever given orders to the morning, or shown the dawn its place, that it might take the earth by the edges and shake the wicked out of it?"

I learned that instead of reactively undoing the damage of the enemy and asking God for help all the time, I was supposed to rise up early (not my flesh's favorite thing to do) and actually command the day to do very specific things for me. I learned to pre-emptively shake all forms of wickedness and darkness from my day, commanding them to cease their enterprises in my life. As I continued this practice, I, for example, started to see my kids be more obedient and cooperative. Instead of being blindsided by all kinds of unforeseen circumstances, my daily life had a smoother flow with less drama. My productivity started improving and I wasn't as flustered and upset as I used to be. This praying, slaying, and reigning stuff really, truly works! And you, dear Friend are on your way there too, in Jesus' mighty name!

## What We've Discovered So Far

Let's go over the basics of what we have discovered regarding the purpose of man. Then, we will tie it into the principles of prevailing in prayer effectively.

- ❖ We were created in the very image and likeness of God (Genesis 1:27).
- ❖ We have free will (Ephesians 2:8-9).
- ❖ Humans were created as spirit beings first. We live in physical bodies and have living souls. (Genesis 1:27).
- ❖ God is the Creator of this world but never meant to personally rule it Himself in this dispensation (Mark 12:1-9, Genesis 14:19, Psalm 115:16).
- ❖ We were created to rule over everything on the earth for God. We were created to be stewards or landlords over the earth to increase, subdue, maintain and beautify the earth under God's authority. (Genesis 14:19, Psalm 115:16).
- ❖ We were created to do all these things while enjoying a loving communicative relationship with our God. (This is where Prevailing Prayer comes into play.)
- ❖ Only human beings and earthly creatures have the right to legally be here on Earth (Colossians 1:9-14). Other spirit beings (good and bad) visit the earth realm and influence activities through physical beings (Ephesians 6:12, Hebrews 1:14, 1 Peter 5:8)
- ❖ Because of Adam and Eve's disobedience, they were driven from the Garden of Eden (Genesis 3:24). They inadvertently gave away our dominion by disobeying God and we have been reduced to a shell of our original design with many of our spiritual abilities severely limited.
- ❖ Original sin (inherited from Adam and Eve) created a separation between God and man, introduced death to man,

- and destroyed many of the spiritual abilities we possessed (Romans 5:12-21).
- ❖ Satan is now the Prince or Ruler of this earth—not man, not God—and the earth is under his control (John 12:31).
- ❖ Jesus made it possible to reunite us with God. We are also restored into right standing (or righteousness) with Him if we accept His Lordship and exercise the needed principles to operate at our originally intended levels. (Colossians 1:20).
- ❖ We can only walk in the fullness of our originally intended levels if and only if we are fully engaged with Christ through the Word, the Holy Spirit, and Power of God and effective prayer. We can only really align ourselves with God and be His instruments in the earth through effective prayer. Prevailing prayer is the magnet that holds all the other pieces (the Word, the Holy Spirit, and the Power of God) of right standing with God together praying, slaying, and reigning is what allows us to exhibit all the attributes of our original purpose

## THOUGHTS AND TIPS ON PRAYER EXECUTION

1. If God was coming to personally visit you in your garden in the cool of the day, how would you prepare for that encounter? How would you host that event? What would you say?
2. Since you now know that you were originally created to have dominion, dress your garden, and subdue the earth how is your prayer life going to reflect these commands?
3. What fruit could you be eating now that still invite defeat, stagnation or separation from God and death into your life? Ask the Holy Spirit to show you those things and disconnect yourself from them. Pray for their effects on you to be neutralized.
4. Since you are created to rule and have dominion, how does this affect your praying style and posture? Are you commanding and subduing like a king?

## Prayer Points

- Lord, you created me for your good pleasure. Let my life please you, I pray.
- Abba Father, you created me and gave me this life. I lift up every aspect of my life into your hands. I ask for grace to be a good steward of the things you have put in my hands to manage, no matter my current situation is now.
- Holy Spirit, I pray that you show me how to willfully co-operate with you.
- Father, by the power of the Holy Spirit, show me how to reclaim and exercise my lost delegated authority.
- Holy Spirit, open my eyes and ears to comprehend why you created me and take up my part in fulfilling your mandate for putting me on this earth.
- Father, even as you worked in collaboration with Adam in the garden, I pray that you show me how to partner with you in every area of my life.
- Lord Jesus, show me how to recognize the works of the Devil and to halt the gates of Hell from encroaching upon my life in Jesus' name.
- Holy Spirit empower me to destroy the works of darkness in my life and in my family.
- I take my authority as a spirit-led child of God and by the revelation of Christ in my life to command my morning and life in Jesus' name.

CHAPTER 5

# KINGDOM KEYS FOR PREVAILING PRAYER

*"The seeking of the Kingdom of God is the chief business of the Christian life." – Jonathan Edwards.*

*Dear Lord, I choose to partner with you to bring your Kingdom into this earth–this earthen vessel called my body and my life, as well as into the planet Earth as a whole. Please show me how to effectively use the keys of the Kingdom to gain access, control, authority and power to the praise and glory of your name! Amen.*

The Kingdom of God is a vast topic woven throughout the entire fabric of the Bible and it continues to be played out right under our very noses. The very shortened version of it goes like this. God, who is the only self-existing eternal King, creates all the universes and heavenly beings including angels. As King, He has all power and subjects who serve Him in eternity.

A third, led by Lucifer or Satan, decide to seize power from God and take over. They are of course, foiled, and thrown out of the third heavens, where God's throne and paradise are. They are nevertheless not all sent to Hell immediately but some are relegated to Earth, its atmosphere and the invisible second heavens and allowed to continue their rebellious activities in the hopes of expanding Satan's power and influence. Consequently, they continue to have smaller skirmishes with God's angels in these different territories.

While Satan is truly no match for God (we know that the fight has been fixed) and the good guys ultimately win, The Kingdom of God will ultimately culminate in the full restoration of God as King of the entire universe. Satan, Hell and the grave will finally be conquered and cast into the lake of fire (Rev. 20:10, 14).

Despite Satan's impending total defeat, even to this day, the quest for kingdom expansion continues to be foremost on the minds of both God and Satan. Each side continues to struggle for greater dominance over the souls of men to push their respective agendas on Earth and ultimately to gain more power over the other side. God created humans purposely designed in His image and with His abilities (including free will and dominion) with the express intent of expanding His Kingdom's rule through them at a satellite location called Earth. We were created as ambassadors or tenants to manage Earth and were given full power, rights, and responsibilities to manage Earth in God's stead and in partnership with Him. Satan scored a big win by deceitfully talking Adam and Eve out of their power and rights as God's Ambassadors, assumed that power and is now the prince of this world (Eph. 2:2, John 16:11, John 14:30). God, being all-knowing, already had a masterplan way of escape in the person of the complete God, complete Man Jesus the Christ. Satan is engaged in an all-out warfare to keep man not just powerless and separated from God, but ignorant of what is rightfully ours through the finished work of Christ as will be discussed in Chapter 7, "Christ In Me, The Hope of Glory" and the transfer of His power to us, His chosen people.

The knowledge of what is rightfully ours, the acquisition of God's power and ultimately using that power through prevailing prayer is exactly what is at stake for the expansion of the Kingdom of God, a concept that was very important during Jesus' time and was actively anticipated. Here are a few more pre-requisite things to know about the Kingdom.

## The Kingdom of God in our Individual Lives

In this earthly realm, God's Kingdom first starts in our own individual lives. This explains why Jesus said that Kingdom is within us:

> And when he was demanded of the Pharisees, when the Kingdom of God should come, he answered them and said, The Kingdom of God cometh not with observation: Neither shall they say, Lo here! or, lo there! *for, behold, the Kingdom of God is within you.* (Luke 17:20-21, KJV).

## The Kingdom of God in the church

Kingdom of God's territory on Earth next extends to the church or *ecclesia* (Greek word) as a whole. The church is made up of individual people who have come to the spiritual revelation of Jesus as the Christ and who are ruled and directed by Christ. Jesus made this clear to His apostle, Simon Peter in the Scripture below that His church would be built on the *rock of individual revelation of Himself to the Believer*:

> "But what about you?" he asked. "Who do you say I am?" Simon Peter answered, "You are the Messiah, the Son of the living God." Jesus replied, "Blessed are you, Simon son of Jonah, for this was not revealed to you by flesh and blood, but by my Father in heaven. And I tell you that you are Peter, and on this rock, I will build my church (Matt. 16:15-18a, NIV).

The church grows upon the spiritual revelation of Jesus as the Christ. The true church is God's primary representative on Earth and is the organized means by which God accomplishes many things on Earth. The church is a living organism, or body, that is ruled by Christ who is the head: "He is the head of the body, the church." Colossians 1:18a (KJV). The head houses the brain or command center of operations for the body and by the same virtue, Jesus is the head of the church and He directs the whole body which is made of many different parts or members:

> "Just as a body, though one, has many parts, but all its many parts form one body, so it is with Christ." (1 Cor. 12:12, KJV).

Being a spiritual and physical part of the church (body) of Jesus is of vital importance because no one is capable of flourishing long-term by themselves in isolation from the body. We need the different giftings of the Holy Spirit filled church as a whole for the common good (1 Cor.12:7, NIV) in order to be fully equipped and edified. We sell ourselves short when we are not involved in a ministry that actively pursues and practices the gifts of the Spirit, and allows the operation of the five-fold ministries: apostles, prophets, evangelists, pastors, and teachers (Eph. 4:11).

## ON EARTH AS IT IS IN HEAVEN

Since God is eternal, His Kingdom in Heaven is also eternal: it has always been, and it will always continue to be. However, here on Earth, a time will come when the lease that was given to Adam will expire and Jesus Christ, the second Adam, will reign on Earth with the saints for a thousand years (Revelation 20:4). So, we see that when Jesus instructed us to pray for His Kingdom to come and His will to be done on Earth as it is in Heaven (Matthew 6:9-13), He is referring to both a more immediate and on-going spiritual arrival and a later physical arrival on Earth. The very fact that in the Lord's Prayer Jesus instructed us to ask for the Kingdom to come is evidence that God's rule in our lives and in the world as a whole is dependent in part on our prayers.

## Laws of the Kingdom

Finally, the Kingdom of God refers to a system of laws and conventions (accepted ways of doing things) by which things function or operate in Heaven. It is worth noting that in the Lord's Prayer (Matthew 6:9-13) He referred to God as "Our Father who is in heaven" and immediately proceeded to pray for "the Kingdom to come and the will of God to be done on Earth as it is heaven."

It is almost impossible to separate the Kingdom of God from the Will of God because in God's Kingdom (Heaven) the system of laws and conventions are all in line with what the King wants, allows and wills (also known as the Will of God). The will of God is covered exhaustively in Chapter 6 but we cannot ever forget that the will of God is ultimately an expression of the way things work in the Kingdom of God.

For example, we know that in Heaven there is no crying, death, sickness, poverty, sin or any other type of disorder:

> Then I saw "a new heaven and a new Earth," for the first heaven and the first Earth had passed away, and there was no longer any sea. I saw the Holy City, the new Jerusalem, coming down out of heaven from God, prepared as a bride beautifully dressed for her husband. And I heard a loud voice from the throne saying, "Look! God's dwelling place is now among the people, and he will dwell with them. They will be his people, and God himself will be with them and be their God. *'He will wipe every tear from their eyes. There will be no more death or mourning or crying or pain, for the old order of things has passed away."* (Rev. 21:1-4, NIV).

When we pray aligned with the Kingdom, we reject everything that is not of the Kingdom: the old order of the world has to be submerged under the conventions or system of God's Kingdom. We instead enforce God's purposes, desires, plans, and command the Kingdom of God to materialize in our human conditions.

## KINGDOM COMES ABOUT THROUGH PRAYER

Jesus had a robust prayer life which drew the disciples to ask Him to teach them to pray. Most of us are familiar with the Lord's prayer:

> After this manner, therefore, pray ye: Our Father which art in heaven, Hallowed be thy name.[10] *Thy kingdom come,* thy will be done on Earth, as it is in heaven. (Matt. 6:9-10, KJV).

After a quick word of praise to our Heavenly Father (hallowed be thy name) Jesus' first priority is to ask for God's will to be done on Earth as it is in Heaven. Why, dear reader? Because as we discussed in the God's Purpose for Creating Man, God can do little to nothing on Earth without our prayers and our cooperation. The Kingdom of God on Earth materializes through prayer and then action aligned with God's instructions. Even though it is true that God is sovereign and can bring in His kingdom without us, He desires, and commands, each of us to ask for it and be a part of the process of bringing in His Kingdom. Prayer then, is the machinery by which God's kingdom comes to fruition in the earth realm.

As we discovered in the meaning of the word prevail, one connotation refers to the ability to use persuasion successfully. When we pray, we plead our case to the Lord. But if we really want to get results, we have to make the correlation between what we are asking for and the advancement of His kingdom. If you are sick for example, your petition to the Father has to persuasively state the case for why your healing is going to help further His Kingdom or agenda. He needs your body to work properly so when He asks you to take food to the homeless man on the corner and share Jesus with Him, for example, you will be able to physically do so and bring glory to Him. **What we are petitioning, declaring, and enforcing all ultimately have to further God's kingdom here on Earth.** Prevailing prayer isn't meant to simply make us feel better; what we are asking for has to tie back to what is of the utmost importance to God: the establishment of His Kingdom on Earth.

We will now examine Jesus's earthly ministry specifically through the lens of the Kingdom of God.

## John the Baptist: Prepare the Way

Even before Jesus' ministry took off, John the Baptist, his forerunner had some important introductory things to say about Him and His work. His words are worth re-considering. He preached powerfully to both commoners and the religious elite, telling them of the nearness of the Kingdom of God and its' characteristics.

> In those days came John the Baptist, preaching in the wilderness of Judaea, and saying, *Repent ye: for the kingdom of heaven is at hand...* I indeed baptize you with water unto repentance but he that cometh after me is mightier than I, whose shoes I am not worthy to bear: *he shall baptize you with the Holy Ghost and with fire"* (Matt. 3:1-2, 11, KJV).

With revelation given by the Holy Spirit, John the Baptist foresaw and predicted what Jesus' ministry would entail and how his disciples would operate: under the baptism of the Holy Spirit and fire. John was prophesying and revealing what would make Jesus' ministry and followers different from the already established religious culture of their time. It was and still is the baptism of the Holy Spirit and fire.

John prescribed the need for a shift from book or head knowledge to spiritual rebirth by Holy Ghost and fire baptism so they could participate in the impending arrival of the Kingdom of God. Nothing has changed about these instructions; they are just as valid today as they were back then. We simply can't really participate in the Kingdom of God and its expansion to our fullest capability without a spiritual rebirth and the baptism of the Holy Spirit.

If you are not filled with the Holy Spirit with the evidence of speaking in tongues, don't be afraid to ask the Lord to beautify your spiritual experience with this precious and necessary gift. God wastes nothing and provides nothing just for the heck of it. If this wasn't needful, trust me, it wouldn't be in the Bible.

## JESUS' KINGDOM WORK: TEACHING, PREACHING, HEALING, AND CONFRONTING THE ENEMY WITH POWER

When Jesus Himself did get down to the business of what He was sent on Earth to do, the work of the Kingdom was His only focus. Jesus commanded us to make the Kingdom of God our priority just as it was His ("seek ye first the Kingdom," Matt. 6:33) and He gave clear directives for us to continue preaching and teaching about it. His earthly ministry was characterized mainly by the following four primary areas of Kingdom work: teaching, preaching, healing, and delivering people from demonic activity by casting out devils, of which we are provided several instances:

> [36] You know the message God sent to the people of Israel, announcing the good news of peace through Jesus Christ, who is Lord of all. [37] You know what has happened throughout the province of Judea, beginning in Galilee after the baptism that John preached— [38] how God anointed Jesus of Nazareth with the Holy Spirit and power, and how he went around doing good and healing all who were under the power of (*or oppressed by*) the Devil, because God was with him. (Acts 10:36-38, NIV) (Italics are my addition from KJV).

And

> Then he called his twelve disciples together and gave them power and authority over all devils and to cure diseases. And he sent them to preach the kingdom of God, and to heal the sick. (Luke 9:1-2, KJV).

Most Believers today are familiar with the first three elements of His work (teaching, preaching, and healing) but it's easy to pretend the fourth (confronting the enemy) isn't there in our Bibles and especially when the Devil has done such a great job of convincing most of the world of his non-existence. Well, Satan is very real as Chapter 9: Enter The Dragon elaborates. Confronting the enemy

*Prevailing Prayer*

has everything to do with exercising God's power which is greater than the Devil's and using it bring successful deliverance from or cessation of demonic activity.

This fourth element of His ministry is still very much a part of the Great Commission that Jesus still expects us to fulfill the whole commission and He basically equated the work of spiritual warfare with a relevant and necessary component of the Kingdom of God.

> But if I cast out devils by the Spirit of God, then the Kingdom of God is come unto you. (Matt. 12:28, KJV).

Jesus clearly expressed and demonstrated that a key element of Kingdom work entails confronting the Devil by binding the works of the enemy or casting out (or slaying) demons and/or demonic activity. Therefore, we need to understand that confronting and overcoming the demonic world is an inseparable part of the work of the Kingdom of God. This is the bulk of "slay" referred to in the over-arching name of this ministry <u>Pray, Slay and Reign,</u> and of which this book Prevailing Prayer is only the first book in the series. The action word "slay" primarily means to kill by violence, to destroy, extinguish, or murder. Slaying refers to spiritual warfare and often brings about a specific area of ministry is often referred to as "deliverance" but it isn't only relegated to Catholic exorcist priests as popular horror movies would have us believe. In this information age, many Believers are finding relevant prayer material to undergo self-deliverance, and most times, they aren't the super-spooky supernatural activities we see take place in movies.

I have come to learn over the years that many of our circumstances seem unaffected by traditional three dimensional prayer alone because we are not acknowledging or addressing the potential involvement of evil manifested by things like the demonic activity, evil strongholds, curses, witchcraft, demonic oppression and even outright possession. All these examples fall under the broad umbrella of the works of darkness that must be subdued and dealt with in spiritual warfare.

Dear Friend, have you noticed evil family patterns that are being perpetuated in your life? Perhaps alcoholism, uncontrollable lying or stealing? Maybe your life a life marked by a series of extremes in evil occurrences, bad luck, chronic inability to move past poverty, inexplicable losses, untimely deaths, etc. and these circumstances remain resistant to positive change despite all your prayers and best efforts? You absolutely want to ask the Lord to show you any secrets you need to know, what and how you should be praying in order to put a permanent end to the issue, instead of allowing it to go unchecked in your life and in the lives of future generations.

Spiritual warfare is such a vast topic with so many unique scenarios that ideally you should be working with a qualified Holy Spirit filled spiritual leader who is well-versed in this area of work to provide the right kind of prayer guidance and support in a strategic prayer and deliverance approach. Please check my website [www.prayslayandreign.com](www.prayslayandreign.com) for more resources specifically regarding prayer consultations as the first step in this process. Unfortunately, there are many Christian leaders today who have zero knowledge of warfare and deliverance. They would even like to convince you this area of work is unnecessary or no longer even real; that it is outdated and a misunderstood area that medications alone can now handle. Trust me, the lack of knowledge and power to deal with an ancient enemy doesn't suddenly negate his existence or the depth of evil in his essence or the hatred he continues to harbor toward us humans. The next chapter deals specifically about Satan but for the purposes of this chapter, an understanding of Jesus' approach to his works through the perspective of the Kingdom is very important to us today, if indeed we want to be in His Kingdom as well.

Prevailing prayer, both for ourselves and for others, inevitably will require some form of spiritual warfare. Who are we prevailing over? The Devil, his team of wicked angels, the corrupted systems of this world as well as our own flesh. Our thoughts are often the first area of attack, closely followed by the suggestive influences of the world and made by others to us. This is why in the introduction, I cautioned vigilance in recognizing and then pulling down rationalizations, and anything else that exults itself against the knowledge of God. We use God's power to pull down these intrusions and then we prevail. Remember that to prevail means to prove to be superior in strength or power or to succeed or win out. Not our own strength, but God's strength:

> [10] Finally, my brethren, be strong in the Lord, and in the power of his might. (Eph. 6:10, KJV).

Let's talk a little bit more then, about the relationship between the kingdom of God, power, and violence.

## THE KINGDOM, POWER, AND VIOLENCE

Ponder over this, dear Reader: is it possible to have a system of government which has no authoritative way of *governing* and enforcing the laws and conventions of that land over its' people? There is no true governmental system, earthly or spiritual that can successfully operate without some form of power or control. What kind of bona fide, ruling king is powerless and therefore helpless? How would that king protect and maintain his kingship? The result of such a scenario would be utter chaos because in the absence of power, there would be no way of checking evil doers and lawlessness, and there would certainly be no king for long.

By the same virtue, there is no Kingdom of God without the power of God. Picture this: The Omnipotent (All-Powerful) one who wants to expand His Kingdom on Earth calls us His ambassadors (2 Cor. 5:20). We are to occupy (subdue and maintain and multiply or enlarge) till He comes. How are we going to do so without any power? This is the true state of most Christians. We have none of our Master's highest attribute: His power. But Jesus wants us to have power. His ultimate instruction to His disciples was for them to wait in Jerusalem until they were endued with POWER from on high *before* embarking on any outreach mission to anyone else about the good news. (Luke 24:47-49).

When we choose to ignore the Holy Spirit, or refuse the fullness of His being and how He chooses to manifest here on Earth according to the original biblical blueprint we unfortunately, operate at a significant disadvantage because we are powerless. Christians who don't exercise the power of the Lord and aren't partnering with the

Holy Spirit are in effect, at less than full capacity and in a power vacuum. It is infinitely more difficult to walk in victory without the power and authority needed to keep the enemy under our feet. The enemy is under our feet as we depicted in our prayer illustration. He is looking for every opportunity for an uprising.

Little wonder then that Paul later would say:

> *For the Kingdom of God is not a matter of talk but of power.* (1 Cor. 4:20, NIV).

We have a lot of marvelous preaching and teaching going on representing the Kingdom of God but what we really need is His power. Power to heal the sick. Power to speak to mountains, power to keep evil in check. God's power comes from praying as we know the early disciples did in the upper room for some forty days, awaiting the release of the Holy Spirit. We simply can't operate without the power of God and hope to successfully prevail in prayer or in life in general. Our lack of results in prayer due to the absence of power in our lives only make our faith sound hollow and ineffective. Spiritual power, therefore, is something we have to deliberately seek after, just as the entire Kingdom of God must be sought after as discussed earlier.

We wage successful spiritual warfare by dealing with underlying demonic problems for which Jesus has already given us the power to overcome, only if we will educate ourselves and walk in it.

## Kingdom Commercial: Violent Men and Women Needed

As a young Christian in my early teens, the most mind-boggling scriptures I encountered was Matthew 11:12 and it really caused me great angst:

> And from the days of John the Baptist until now the kingdom of heaven suffereth violence, and the violent take it by force. (KJV).

I saw Jesus as the Prince of Peace, the Good Shepherd with the lambs and little children surrounding Him, but I couldn't understand or imagine Him endorsing violence. I remember spending many an afternoon during our mandatory siesta hour in boarding school praying and pondering over this verse. I was a prim and proper Episcopalian (aka Anglican) who had only recently been exposed to the charismatic movement, the concept of being born again and the attendant forceful, powerful expressions of teaching, preaching and ministering. It was truthfully, initially all quite unsettling, but still exciting nevertheless. I wholeheartedly asked Jesus to give me the new birth and sought to learn more about Him and grow in Him. But this one verse just upended everything I thought I knew and understood of Him. How was I supposed to be *violent* in order to capture the kingdom? Did I even have those violent sensibilities in me to take the Kingdom by force? Would I ever even be able to seize and be part of the Kingdom if violence was a pre-requisite?

Over time as I have continued to examine this scripture, I have come to better understand how the intents and purposes and Will of God don't just happen by chance here on Earth. Combined with my increased knowledge about Satan, God's purpose in creating man and the role of prayer in bringing God's Kingdom on Earth, I now realize that we often have to earnestly contend for our faith. We must wrestle in prayer and slay to ultimately have the dominion we were designed to live and reign in. This is how we Pray, Slay, and Reign!"

We have all seen US Army recruiting ads over the years. A very popular and timeless one typically depicts a man wearing a hat with the US flag motif on it, his bony finger pointing out of the poster saying: Uncle Sam Wants You! Well, the Kingdom of God is similarly recruiting for God's soldiers and ideally God is looking for people who will allow themselves to become spiritually violent and skilled warriors to deal with the violent and ever-encroaching aggression of the kingdom of darkness in this world.

Somewhere in the passage of time, the traditional church has become so sensitized to Jesus being the Gentle Jesus, Meek and Mild, the very epitome of the God of Love who doesn't want anyone to perish, that we have successfully lost sight of Him being the God of War. Exodus 15:3 (KJV) says that, "The Lord is a man of war." Another powerful verse says:

> The LORD shall go forth as a mighty man, he shall stir up jealousy like a man of war: he shall cry, yea, roar; he shall prevail against his enemies. (Isaiah 42:13, KJV).

Our Leader, our Captain who leads His armies both heavenly and earthly, is still a mighty warrior. He is still great in battle and Jehovah is His name. That part of God and the ministry of Jesus has been conveniently covered up by the Devil because he doesn't want the Believer to know there is that very dangerous side of Jesus and that ultimately neither He nor we Believers are pansies to be messed with.

Royal Prayer Warriors need a violent mindset in prayer when it comes to dealing with the works of darkness. I am referring specifically to the spirits behind the problem and not the people themselves who might be used as a pawn. We don't have the luxury of coddling evil spirits and situations all in the name of love. In fact, a closer look at Jesus quickly dispels the myth of Him being all warm and fuzzy and loving when it came to the ruling religious leaders. He barely tolerated the Pharisees, calling them a "brood of evil vipers", "whitewashed tombstones", literal "children of the Devil" and physically drove out the money-changers. In fact, based on how often He was at odds with them, was nearly stoned or pushed off a cliff (John 8:59, Matt. 26:4) it's amazing how he managed to stay alive and preach for three long years at all!

## EMBRACING EVERYTHING THAT THE KINGDOM ENTAILS

Many Christians are living on less than their full rights because they misunderstand this critical component of Jesus' work and His plan for His followers. We are therefore losing many battles we should be winning because we don't have our full set of tools at our disposal. If we want to experience Heaven (the Kingdom of God) on Earth, right here in our own lives, we need to embrace everything that the kingdom entails. This unequivocally includes the experience of walking and living in the Spirit. We cannot afford to conveniently cross out the areas that aren't to our taste, understanding or comfort level. We could very well be ultimately inviting the rejection of the very Lord Jesus we claim to be serving:

## What God has Shown Me: In Closing

In conclusion, The Kingdom of God is the only gospel Jesus preached and the only one we can cling to if we have any hope of seeing our prayers answered and living victorious Christian lives. In Chapter 9, Enter The Dragon we will learn more details about the Devil, his operations, and strategies which combined with other information covered in this book will allow us effectively slay and reign.

In our dispensation, if we want to experience victory in our lives, we have to align yourself with the prescribed conventions that allow the Kingdom of God to flourish in our lives. On the topic of experiential baptism of the Holy Spirit and fire, by faith we have to grasp the spiritual truths in the Word about it, and then appropriate it for ourselves. The Holy Spirit is easier caught than taught. I recommend spending time in fellowships which teach and practice this discipline.

## Thoughts and Tips on Prayer Execution

1. Which elements of the Kingdom are missing and most pertinent to your going to the next dimension of your prayer experience?
2. How do you intend to seek those things into manifestation?
3. If you already have these elements in your life, how can they be strengthened to take you even higher and make you even more powerful?

## Prayer Points

- Lord, as much as I am pre-occupied with my immediate needs, help me to see the bigger picture and seek your Kingdom first. Show me how to pray mutually beneficial prayers that will expand your Kingdom.
- Father, give me the grace to seek and put your Kingdom first.
- Forgive me, Abba for where I have rejected your whole counsel I pray.
- Holy Spirit, baptize and fill me with your very essence.
- Let the same power that filled Jesus be my portion in the mighty name of Jesus I pray.
- Holy Spirit, equip me with your strength and stamina to wrestle in prayer
- Father, you describe yourself as a Man of War. Show me how to emulate you in this area.

## CHAPTER 6

# WORK THE WORD & WILL HIS WILL INTO YOUR WORLD

*"The word of God is the food by which prayer is nourished and made strong." – E. M. Bounds*

*Holy Spirit, I ask that the necessity of your Word and your Will are not lost on me. Let your Word be written on the tablet of my heart. May these general concepts and specific revelations for different situations in my life catapult my prayer life and overall Christian life into new dimensions. Thank you, Abba. Amen.*

### WORK THE WORD

Working the Word of God means reading and or hearing, understanding, and then moving it from the Bible's pages to words on your literal lips that you pray to God. Given what has been examined thus far, it's self-evident that a fundamental component of results-oriented prayer is knowing and understanding the whole Word of God and praying specific, relevant promises in that Word back to Him. The whole Word of God is more than just the promises of God; it includes His instructions, laws, and judgments. Working the Word activates changes in our thinking and behavior, both of which allow us to look more like the reigning people we were originally created to be.

I came to the realization of the importance of working the Word when the Lord opened my eyes on this verse:

> [7] If ye abide in me, and my words abide in you, ye shall ask what ye will, and it shall be done unto you. (John 15:7, KJV).

Ask what you will, and it will be done for you. I knew this verse, and often wondered why I wasn't getting answers when Jesus assured us we could ask what we wanted. There had to be a glitch somewhere. It took a long time for me to realize that even though I was abiding in Him, His Words weren't abiding in me enough; I would have to go to a whole new level of understanding and practicing His Word in me to get to the point where I truly would ask *and* receive. Dear Friend, please step up the level of the Word abiding in you, if you want a prevailing prayer life.

Let's first examine what the Bible has to say about the Word of God; its supremacy, vitality, and inerrancy.

## PART 1
## SUPREMACY OF THE SCRIPTURES

God goes by several names in the Bible and each of those names reflect an essential characteristic of Himself. God is inseparable from His name because since He is an undefiled Spirit Being and we are fallen humans, it's hard for us to grasp who He is without the names which demonstrate aspects of Himself. For example, In Genesis 22:14 Abraham called Him Jehovah Jireh on Mount Moriah because God miraculously provided a ram in the bush as a sacrifice to replace Isaac to prove to Abraham that He God was capable of taking care of all Abraham's needs. God tells Moses to tell Pharaoh that He is the I AM to explain that He is the Self-Existing God who supersedes Pharaoh's own kingship and deity status. Naturally, God places great importance on His name. Nevertheless, God takes His own Word even more seriously and puts it above everything else, including His name. God is as good as His Word. He stakes His reputation on His word. He believes in, respects, and honors His own words so much so that He is even willing to discount His name or character or the very essence of who He is at the expense of His Word, as the second half of this verse tells us:

> [2] I will worship toward Your holy temple and praise Your name for Your loving-kindness and for Your truth *and* faithfulness; for You have exalted above all else Your name and Your word *and* You have magnified Your word above all Your name! (Psalm 138:2, AMPC).

If God feels this way about His own words, it is in our best interest to think like God and highly esteem His words with just as much respect as God does. We gain access to God's hand by presenting His own Words back to Him. And this is why this book is so heavily infused with verses and explanations of verses because the Word will be critical to the manifestation of your prayers.

## Vitality of the Word

The word "vitality" means "exuberant physical strength or mental vigor" and "power to live or grow." Therefore, the vitality of the Scriptures means that the Word has life and power! The Word of God nourishes our spirit man: it is our literal food which gives us strength so we can stand firmly in patience to receive manifestation of our requests to the Lord. There are many verses in both the Old and New Testament that refer to the vitality or life-giving nature of the commands and words of God.

Jesus said:

It is the spirit that quickeneth; the flesh profiteth nothing: *the words that I speak unto you, they are spirit, and they are life.* (John 6:63, KJV).

The wise King Solomon echoed this idea:

*My son, do not forget my teaching, but keep my commands in your heart, for they will prolong your life many years and bring you peace and prosperity... This will bring health to your body and nourishment to your bones.* (Proverbs 3:1, 8, NIV).

Job went a step further to say that the Word of God is even more important than regular food for the physical body, thereby promoting the need for fasting:

Neither have I gone back from the commandment of his lips; *I have esteemed the words of his mouth more than my necessary food.* (Job 23:12, KJV).

## INERRANCY OF THE WORD

Inerrancy refers to the unfailing nature of God's Word. Inerrancy means purity and a lack of error. While we may not yet understand every aspect of the Word and the differing times and contexts within which each writer wrote, it is still in essence, all true. There is no error in it that negates His existence, or the overall truthfulness of His Words:

[5] *Every word of God is pure*: he is a shield unto them that put their trust in him. (Prov. 3:5)

I heard an apt illustration of this concept when someone explained that God can not lie and that if you were wearing a blue dress and God said it was red, by virtue of the power of his uttered or spoken Word that dress would have to become red because He said it was so. The Word of God won't work effectively in us if we don't believe that the Almighty God, creator of everything, spoke those words:

> *All scripture is given by inspiration of God and is profitable for doctrine, for reproof, for correction, for instruction in righteousness: That the man of God may be perfect, thoroughly furnished unto all good works.* (2 Timothy 3:16, KJV).

Here, Paul is telling Timothy that he will not be perfected (or thoroughly equipped) for good works if he doesn't truly believe the scriptures.

<u>Believing</u> and <u>understanding</u> everything in the Bible are not the same thing and they are not interchangeable either. There's a difference between believing and understanding. For example, I believe that the sun will rise in the east in the morning. I can believe this because I see it. I don't have to understand the scientific details of how the earth rotates around the sun, on its axis at a stable rate, how gravity keeps planets in orbit, or how the orbit of the earth causes the change in seasons. It is possible to not understand some parts of the Word of God, but that shouldn't stop us from believing it. God is more than able to bring understanding with time. Believing that the Word is accurate, true, and trustworthy is a non-negotiable in our ability to tap into a prevailing prayer life.

We also need to settle in the very depth of our soul that God's Words are right, accurate and true, that they accomplish what they were designed to do. God doesn't haphazardly change His mind or the intent of His Words. As we make our petitions to the Lord, we must be fully convinced unequivocally that He means what He says and says what He means:

> *God is not a man, that he should lie; neither the son of man, that he should repent: hath he said, and shall he not do it? or hath he spoken, and shall he not make it good?* (Numbers 23:19, KJV).

If we don't believe and continue to believe God's specific promise was intended for our situation, we will not be able to stand in faith to see it come to pass.

> "For my thoughts are not your thoughts, neither are your ways my ways, saith the Lord. For as the heavens are higher than the earth, so are my ways higher than your ways, and my thoughts than your thoughts. For as the rain cometh down, and the snow from heaven, and returneth not thither, but watereth the earth, and maketh it bring forth and bud, that it may give seed to the sower, and bread to the eater: *So shall my word be that goeth forth out of my mouth: it shall not return unto me void, but it shall accomplish that which I please, and it shall prosper in the thing whereto I sent it.*" (Isaiah 55:8-11, KJV).

If we are not convinced beyond a shadow of a doubt of the simple truth of God's Word, and abiding or staying in it, we will not be successful in seeing results. "If you abide in me, and my words abide in you, ask what you will and it will be done for you." John 15:7. It is, after all, the truth that *you* know that will set you free:

> Then said Jesus to those Jews which believed on him, 'If ye continue in my word, then are ye my disciples indeed; [32] And ye shall know the truth, and the truth shall make you free." (John 8:31-32, KJV).

Continuing or abiding in the truth of His Word is therefore critical. We have to remain steadfast in the Word.

## Capture Every Thought Contrary to The Word

In the introduction, we discussed the importance of recognizing and capturing rationalizations and distractions:

We demolish arguments and every pretension that sets itself up against the knowledge of God, and we take captive every thought to make it obedient to Christ. (2 Corinthians 10:5, NIV).

We have to "take captive every thought" because doubts will surface, we will be distracted, and we will begin to question. This is the work of the enemy because he doesn't want us to have vital prayer lives! You should be on the look-out for all the subtle ways these arguments, pretentions, ideologies, worldviews, mindsets etc. permeate our lives and thought processes, even while at the root, they are contrary to God's Word. Most times they are a form of cognitive dissonance, an elaborate lie wrapped up in some element of truth but only the Holy Spirit can bring up those inconsistencies and incongruencies to our attention to be dealt with. The importance of the following scripture in unmasking these inconsistencies:

> "For the word of God is alive and active. Sharper than any double-edged sword, it penetrates even to dividing soul and spirit, joints and marrow; it judges the thoughts and attitudes of the heart." (Hebrews 4:12, NIV)

Ask the Holy Spirit to help you to discern these subtle things that take us astray. The Word of God is powerful! It is sharper than any sword, and in fact, the Word of God is known as the Sword of the Spirit (Ephesians 6:17).

## Part 2

The first part of this chapter was dedicated to knowing and understanding the supremacy, vitality, and inerrancy of the scripture. Now we'll put this important concept into action!

I urge you to be a stickler about working the Word of God. Acquire the Word by reading and/or hearing the Word for personal understanding and illumination. Then, incorporate the Words of God into your prayers by verbalizing His promises:

> "As for me, this is my covenant with them," says the Lord. "My Spirit, who is on you, will not depart from you, and *my words that I have put in your mouth will always be on your lips*, on the lips of your children and on the lips of their descendants—from this time on and forever," says the Lord. (Is. 59:11, NIV).

God says in the above-mentioned scripture that He has a covenant with us. That His Spirit will be in and with us forever if we will always keep His words on our lips. As we keep His words on our lips, it will build our faith as we stand on His promises as we petition our Father.

Therefore, incorporate or work the Word of God into your prayer life by keeping it to memory, making it a part of our stream of consciousness and speaking it out loud. We have to raise its value or estimation in our own hearts to the point where it matters sometimes more than our physical food and it compels us to fast. We have to recognize that our spiritual life, strength, and power all flow from the ingestion of the Word. It is the sap that flows from Jesus the True Vine into our lives, which are His branches (John 15:1-4).

## CHILD-LIKE FAITH IN THE WORD

To effectively Work the Word and Will His Will into Your World, we have to acknowledge the supremacy, vitality, and inerrancy of the Word with a child-like faith (Matthew 18:3). Having a child-like faith doesn't mean completely setting aside our intellect. Nevertheless, many children of God simply do NOT believe the Word of their Father. Yet, Jesus was very clear we will NOT be able to enter and fully reap the benefits of His Kingdom, unless we come with child-like faith. Not child*ish*, but child-*like* faith.

> At the same time came the disciples unto Jesus, saying, "Who is the greatest in the kingdom of heaven?" And Jesus called a little child unto him, and set him in the midst of them, and said, "Verily I say unto you, except ye be converted, and become as little children, ye shall not enter into the kingdom of heaven. Whosoever, therefore, shall humble himself as this little child, the same is greatest in the kingdom of heaven." (Matthew 18:1-4, KJV).

We work the Word by allowing our minds to be converted and humbling ourselves. In other words, we have to submerge our ideologies, quirks, thoughts etc. and allow them to be over-ridden by what the Word says.

## My Testimony

As a precocious pre-teen, I was an avid reader who inadvertently filled my mind with all kinds of worldly ideas that didn't always line up with the Word of God. I considered myself a feminist even at a young age and as an intellectual, I had great trouble accepting some parts of the Bible. For example, I had read verses that seemed to depict women as less than men. I used to think things like "How insulting of God to say the man is the head of the woman, when we women are just as good as men." "God thinks I'm a second-class citizen", etc.

Long before the word "snarky" ever existed, I had a black belt in sarcasm and I'm sure I was crowned the Queen of Snark sometime back in the eighties. I now know this attitude can be a form of unbelief and hardness of heart. In addition to this peculiar trait, I always had an inquiring questioning mind and refused to take most things at face value. I needed to think through things before I accepted them as my own. I had to understand the "why" for myself first. I took pride in not marching to anyone's drum beat and being my own independent thinker who questioned stuff first. All these things, if balanced, tempered, and redirected properly with the Lord's guidance can be used for great good. But if not, they can also erode or even completely obstruct one's child-like faith in the Lord.

Obviously, the more I grew in the Lord, the more I realized that these quirks didn't exactly help in some areas of my own personal Christian walk. Thankfully, the revival and school culture I was in were a conducive environment for displays of Holy Spirit power mixed with spirited intellectual and spiritual discussions. I was also exposed to excellent, biblically sound teaching. Over time, I found it was easier to take things at face value because I already knew the foundational framework within which those new spiritual concepts were being presented.

But I hadn't worked out all my worldly views (yes, this is something we have to keep working on) and when I started dating in college, I wasn't particularly convinced I was supposed to exclusively date born-again Christians specifically. So, for a while I was in a long-distance relationship with a young man who was a great guy, came from a wonderful family that my parents approved of and was a very decent upstanding human being. He didn't agree with nor believe everything I did but we got along well and had a lot in common.

However, within the space of a few months of us talking on the phone, I saw my connection with the Lord suddenly take a nose dive. I woke up one day and it felt like the door of communication and love between the Lord and I just swung shut and He was nowhere to be found. My prayers just hit the ceiling and came right back. I knew something wasn't right. I felt like I had lost my best friend. God had disappeared from me. I sought hard after the Lord. And then after a couple of weeks, He gave me my answer by showing me this scripture very clearly in the Bible.

> [3] But I want you to realize that the head of every man is Christ, and the head of the woman is man, and the head of Christ is God. (1 Corinthians 11:3, NIV).

God spoke to me in my heart and explained that by choosing to date an unbeliever that I was prepared to marry, I was essentially choosing a spiritual head (or covering or umbrella) who was spiritually shorter in stature than I was and was, therefore, stunting my relationship with Him the Father! I was blown away by this simple revelation because it now made perfect sense. It was a verse I had been familiar with, but one that had been somewhat offensive to me because I mistook to mean that as a woman, I wasn't good enough to be the head or that only a man could represent me. I mistook this to mean that by extension, I was a second-class citizen of the Kingdom. And now I knew better.

Some spiritual truths don't make natural sense, but they are still true. They require further prayer and reflection to understand but our upfront obedience even in the absence of our understanding can literally save our lives. I can't begin to describe how quickly I broke that relationship off; I needed no further convincing. I was

*Prevailing Prayer*

out because I wasn't willing to trade my sweet communion with the Lord for a relationship with a guy who didn't check all the boxes God prescribed for me.

We therefore each have a decision to make. Do we want results or not? Do we want to be great and powerful in our Christian walk or not? If we do, then we do have to follow God's system, which is built on His Word. There is no way around it. He expects us to be converted in our minds and accept His word as is, with the help of the Holy Spirit to interpret it for us:

> "And be not conformed to this world: but be ye transformed by the renewing of your mind, that ye may prove what is that good, and acceptable, and perfect, will of God." (Romans 12:2, KJV).

We have to step out in faith and ask the Holy Spirit to transform us by the "renewing of your mind." Our circumstances may be factually accurate because they are our current reality, but they still subject to the Word of God. Our facts are not, under any circumstance, more important, powerful or real than God's Word.

God expects us to rely on the Holy Spirit and to rightly divide the Word of God. It's also important to remind you that the Word of God includes both the Old and New Testaments. We have to accept the Word from beginning to end. To ignore one at the expense of the other is a costly mistake that will rob us of balance and power. Even if we are not sure or convinced completely, we can pray and confess our inadequacies to the Lord. We are to pray to the Lord to help us in our unbelief or lack of understanding and request wisdom and understanding. It is okay to confess our absolute need for His assistance to increase our faith and or understanding in that specific area that is tripping us up.

## Pray God's Word, Not Your Feelings or Circumstances

Rehearsing our problems and feelings to God is not results-oriented prayer. Crying, complaining, moaning, belly-aching, ruminating over our feelings, especially negative feelings, don't particularly count in the grand scheme of things when it comes to getting answers from God. If this is what moved the hand of God on our behalf, the whole world would be one loud wailing party. While there is a need to recognize and acknowledge our problems, we have to move past simply airing our grievances to God and give Him something to work with to get the desired changes we wish to see. What truly moves God is His own Word, prayed back to Him.

The whole physical world as we know it appeared by the articulation or declaration of God's Word and your desired world will also appear by your declaration of His Word. If we will pray God's promises back to Him, His Words, which are spirit, will eventually come alive and be manifested and become real in our physical world. *Knowing* what the mind of God is concerning your specific situation and standing on that Word to make one's case to the Lord is what then sets things in motion for answered prayer. This is why it is absolutely important every child of God seek the face of God by studying and meditating on His word about our specific situations.

Here is a biblical example of this principle. In this excerpt, we learn that Abraham did not pay attention to or bellyache about all the adverse circumstances surrounding his barrenness (i.e. their ages and Sarah's barrenness.)

> (As it is written, I have made thee a father of many nations,) before him whom he believed, even God, who quickeneth the dead, and calleth those things which be not as though they were. Who against hope believed in hope, that he might become the father of many nations, *according to that which was spoken, So shall thy seed be.* And being not weak in faith, he considered not his own body now dead, when he was about an hundred years old, neither yet the deadness of Sarah's womb: He staggered not at the promise of God through unbelief; but was strong in faith, giving glory to God; And being fully persuaded that, what he had promised, he was able also to perform. (Rom. 4:17-21, KJV).

He had the option to dwell on his negative circumstances and to complain about them to God in prayer. But instead, we see that Abraham was fully convinced or persuaded about the promise God had given him. Abraham stood on "that which was spoken" i.e. the promise He had been given and presented those words back to God, being fully persuaded God was able to deliver what He had already promised. And thus, Father Abraham got his prayer, his deepest and most pressing desire answered, and Isaac manifested in real life.

We see then, that while the facts, (or the flesh) may be accurate, they are temporary, not permanent. But God's Word is eternal.

## In Conclusion on Working the Word

See with Spiritual Not Natural Eyes: Many people give more credence to what their natural senses tell them than what the Word of God says. This is actually a subversion or inversion of the way a born-again spiritual person is supposed to process their circumstances: "we walk by faith and not by sight." (2 Cor. 5:7.) We also make the mistake of only believing what we can see, or we want God to manifest Himself physically in some way to "prove" Himself before we'll put our faith in Him.

We are required to have faith in what God says first and then we get to see it come to pass in the natural. God's permanent Word can and will eventually supersede the reality or facts on the ground if we will call His Word, Will, Intent, and Truth to come into being. God's Word is always the ultimate truth. God's Word is permanent and will never fail. (Matt. 24:35).

For any Christian who wants an effective prayer life, the importance of working the Word of God ranks above all else because God counts it of the utmost importance. If you are going to unleash the royal prayer warrior within, you absolutely have to speak the Word of the King. You have to carry yourself with the same decorum as your Father and speak your Father's Words. You must be willing to decree things, just like your dad the King does. You will see that over time, your words coming out of your mouth will carry weight too. Your words will have the ability to prevail. Your words will dominate. Your words will prove superior in strength, power, and influence. You will amaze yourself!

## THE WILL OF GOD

Closely tied to the *Word of God* is the *Will of God*. When we speak of the Will of God, we are referring to things that are approved, acceptable and sanctioned by God in Heaven because of their conformity to His nature and/or plans. Paul admonishes the Body of Christ with the following words:

> "And be not conformed to this world: but be ye transformed by the renewing of your mind, that ye may prove what is that good, and acceptable, and perfect, will of God." (Romans 12:2, KJV).

We get to taste or "prove" the perfect will of God when we have renewed minds by the Word of God. The Will of God is revealed in His Word, which then again shows us why the understanding and application of His Word is so vital to our ability to have a productive prayer life. The Will of God refers to His intent, purpose or choice: they are good (not evil) and acceptable (appropriate) things in the mind of God that will ultimately align and unite us with Him, as opposed to taking us further away from Him.

There's often a lot of confusion regarding God's will and this trips up many believers who aren't sure whether or not they are asking correctly. They fear they may be requesting something God doesn't want them to have. Many of these questions can be answered by a greater understanding of the Word of God, because the Word of God shows His intent, which is another word for His will. According to the Word of God, if we ask in line with God's Will, we are guaranteed an answer or our petitions are granted:

> "And this is the confidence that we have in him, that, *if we ask any thing according to his will, he heareth us*: And if we know that he hear us, whatsoever we ask, we know

that we have the petitions that we desired of him." (1 John 5:14-15, KJV).

As Romans 12:2 states there is the *perfect* Will of God as opposed to the *permissive will of God*. Within the realm of the perfect will of God, anything that concerns wholeness, peace, joy, righteousness, goodness, health, and at least a level of success and general economic self-sufficiency is NEVER outside the perfect will of God. Consider these verses which make it clear that success, prosperity or wholeness and obedience to God with everything within us:

> Beloved, I pray that in every way you may succeed *and* prosper and be in good health [physically], just as [I know] your soul prospers [spiritually]. (1 John 3:2, AMP)

And

> You will again obey the Lord and follow all his commands I am giving you today. *Then the Lord your God will make you most prosperous in all the work of your hands and in the fruit of your womb, the young of your livestock and the crops of your land. The Lord will again delight in you and make you prosperous, just as he delighted in your ancestors,* if you obey the Lord your God and keep his commands and decrees that are written in this Book of the Law and turn to the Lord your God with all your heart and with all your soul. (Deut.30:8-10, NIV).

Conversely, we know that the enemy, also known as the adversary (the one who opposes) has the opposite agenda:

> "The thief does not come except to steal, and to kill, and to destroy. I have come that they may have life, and that they may have *it* more abundantly." (John 10:10, NIV).

Based on the first half of this verse, it could be tempting to simplistically assume that if anything seems difficult or painful then God isn't in it. However, God's perfect Will could be the more difficult choice that often requires stripping, pruning or some sort of loss.

The difference between God's and the Devil's will is their diametrically opposed end results: God's goal is life more abundantly. Satan's goal is death and permanent separation from God. Since Chapter 9 Enter the Dragon, Know Your Adversary talks more about Satan and our fallen world, I will not belabor the point here other than to say anything that ultimately separates us from God, steals, brings death or destruction to good things typically trace back to our enemy whose sole desire on Earth is to perpetuate separation from God and our ultimate demise in Hell with him.

In the permissive will of God, God allows people to get what they want, even though it isn't necessarily His very best option for them.

There are natural consequences to every decision we make, good or bad, and it is the same for spiritual decisions. Being in God's permissive will always makes us more susceptible to the enemy's attacks. Being in God's perfect will provides a natural hedge of protection that disobedience and living in His permissive will could compromise. This is why Solomon says:

> Whoever digs a pit may fall into it; whoever breaks through a wall *(or hedge as per KJV)* may be bitten by a snake.[9] Whoever quarries stones may be injured by them; whoever splits logs may be endangered by them. (Eccl. 10:8 NIV).

Given these realities, if we are forced into a situation that puts us in the permissive will of God, we have to be aware of the potential consequences and be prepared to prayerfully counteract those things from happening or even if they do, minimizing those liabilities. As mentioned before, Satan looks for every opportunity to exploit our weaknesses or lapses to his advantage.

Father Abraham provides a great example of the issue at stake here. In Genesis 13, Abraham and Lot grew so rich that they were forced to separate so their respective herdsmen wouldn't be so stretched for pasture for their livestock. Abraham allowed his nephew to select where he wanted to go first. Lot chose to go pitch his tent closer to Sodom, even though he knew they were "wicked and sinners before the Lord exceedingly" (verse 13). I believe Abraham knew exactly what was at stake and was prepared to act in case of worst case scenario on behalf of his nephew. Indeed, his watchful preparedness and willingness to spring into action saved his nephew twice, as we discussed in chapter 3 The Perils of Prayerlessness. I believe God blessed Abraham with his son Isaac partly because He saw how wonderful a father Abraham would be, based in part on the way he watched spiritually over his nephew Lot. Abraham covered his nephew and showed God his ability to be a real father way before Ishmael or Isaac came on the scene.

Another example of the permissive will of God is found in 1 Sam. 8:1-22. The children of Israel decided they were tired of a theocracy and wanted to be like other nations. The prophet Samuel was particularly grieved by what He saw as a rejection of God. Apparently, God agreed with Him, but He still allowed their request to be granted, even while warning them of its negative consequences which have been italicized below:

> Samuel told all the words of the LORD to the people who were asking him for a king. He said, "*This is what the king who will reign over you will claim as his rights*: He will take your sons and make them serve with his chariots and horses, and they will run in front of his chariots. Some he will assign to be commanders of thousands and commanders of fifties, and others to plow his ground and reap his harvest, and still others to make weapons of war and equipment for his chariots. He will take your daughters to be perfumers and cooks and bakers. *He will take the best of your fields and vineyards and olive groves and give them to his attendants. He will take a tenth of your grain and of your vintage and give it to his officials and attendants. Your male and female servants and the best of your cattle and donkeys he will take for his own use. He will take a tenth of your flocks, and you yourselves will become his slaves. When that day comes, you will cry out for relief from the king you have chosen, but the LORD will not*

*answer you in that day."* But the people refused to listen to Samuel. "No!" they said. "We want a king over us. Then we will be like all the other nations, with a king to lead us and to go out before us and fight our battles." (1 Samuel 8:10-18, NIV).

In essence, God told them there would be a new economic and social class system. Social inequality would arise as a result of their choice to have a human king. God was telling them there would be an unfair system of taxation necessary to support the existence of a king and his family. They would no longer be in a somewhat socio-egalitarian society.

In the end, God's perfect Will better aligns with His much-beloved business of adding more good stuff spiritually to us, after all He sent us Jesus so we could have life and life more abundantly (John 10:10).

> Every branch in me that beareth not fruit he taketh away: and every branch that beareth fruit, he purgeth it, *that it may bring forth more fruit.* (John 15:2, KJV).

When we partner with God, He takes away things that cause fruitlessness because they hinder our spiritual growth by taking away much-needed food and resources from the other parts of the tree. He also stimulates and encourages the things that do bear fruit to do so even more.

Something in our carnal nature literally has to be given up in order for us to gain something supernatural and spiritual, even as Jesus had to give up His earthly life to be resurrected. This explains why Jesus wrestled between God the Father's perfect Will and His own request for God's permissive will in prayer at the Garden of Gethsemane (Matthew 26:36-46). The prospect of the overwhelmingly physical pain of the crucifixion was so very real that He asked the Father if there was possibly another way to still get the same result, while emphasizing "Nevertheless not my will, but yours".

The burden is always on us to ascertain and recognize God's Will and submerge our natural will under His Will. We have to discern between God's perfect and permissive Will, as well as the possibility of completely venturing outside of both by listening to the Devil. We know the hallmark of the enemy's handiwork is to ultimately detract, hinder, subtract or steal from us, to destroy, kill or any such related activities that move us further away from God and closer under his evil control. It is obviously in our best interest to be alert and combat these things in our lives whenever they occur.

## Man's Free Will versus God's Will

God created us to have our own free will. In matters great and small, there is no occasion where God ever forces us to choose His will instead of our own. This part of the beauty of understanding God's great love, His purpose for creating man, and the kind of love God wants reciprocated back to Him. God wants us to choose Him, His way, His Will. Anything else outside of free will, and we are "robots" programmed to respond to God's commands. That is not what God wanted. We were all created with our own individual will. God truly respects our willingness to submerge ourselves in His and be taught to prefer his Will. Answered prayer then, flows from a submerged will, and a life that actively asks for the things that please God by being in the Will of God:

Teach me to do thy will; for thou art my God: thy spirit is good; lead me into the land of uprightness (Psalm 143:10, KJV).

## The Will versus the Timing of God

There are two things under this section I wish to address. The first is that it is possible to know the Will of God but be out of alignment in the timing of that will. We may be premature or late in the timing of the manifestation of God's Perfect Will for our lives. We therefore have to be careful not to out of step with God when it comes to timing. As always, prayer is important for discernment. Take Esau for example, who was Jacob's older twin and technically supposed to inherit the blessing of the birthright.

> Make every effort to live in peace with everyone and to *be holy; without holiness, no one will see the Lord...* See

that no one is sexually immoral, or is *godless like Esau, who for a single meal sold his inheritance rights as the oldest son. Afterward, as you know, when he wanted to inherit this blessing, he was rejected. Even though he sought the blessing with tears, he could not change what he had done.* (Hebrews 12:14, 16, 17, KJV).

In this excerpt, Paul explains that Esau was godless and unholy. When he eventually realized the evil of his ways, it was too late for him to be restored to his original place as the first-born son with the blessing of the birthright.

In Genesis 25:23, God foretold Rebecca, the mother of these twins, that before Esau was born that Esau would forfeit his birthright to his younger brother, Jacob. True to God's Word, Esau grew up to be a profane man, who married idol-worshipping women and caused his parents much grief with his choices. He verbally gave his brother Jacob permission to have his birthright as the first-born son, even though he really had no intention of honoring his word (Gen. 25:29-34). But through a well-orchestrated but back-handed conspiracy between Jacob and Rebecca, Esau was officially deprived of his father's blessing, which Jacob took.

In this example, we see Esau disqualified himself from God's perfect will and the traditional order because of his choices and lifestyle, even though he later repented and came back to himself. Eventually, God in His great mercy, gave him another chance. Esau became a powerful man in his own right but he missed the window of opportunity to have the birthright that was truly his and the transaction was non-refundable, even though God restored him in other ways.

Secondly, most believers assume when they are not getting their answers after a while then it automatically means they weren't praying in line with God's Will. This isn't necessarily the truth. There are many verses and parables that emphasize praying for a long time without giving up and no mention is made of praying outside of God's will in those verses. For example, in the Parable of the Persistent Widow, Jesus starts by saying:

> That men should always pray and not give up. (Luke 18:1-8, NIV)

He then ends the parable by musing out loud:

> "And will not God bring about justice for his chosen ones, who cry out to him day and night? Will he keep putting them off? I tell you, he will see that they get justice, and quickly. However, when the Son of Man comes, will he find faith on the earth?" (Luke 18:7-8, NIV).

We see that praying persistently, even in the absence of results, is not an indication we are praying outside the Will of God. In fact, God is immensely impressed by our ability to continue to persist in prayer. The litmus test for knowing if we are praying in the Will of God isn't how quickly it gets answered. Timing is not necessarily a factor in determining if something is the Will of God—think about how long it took Sarah and Abraham to have Isaac. We know we are praying the Will of God because we have sought His face to thoroughly know and understand His particular stance for our specific lives and trust that God will bring our prayers into manifestation regardless of how long it will take. We then wrestle in prayer for its manifestation until the Holy Spirit tells us it's okay to no longer pray for it.

I also want to add that even if we seemingly aren't getting a specific prayer request answered, God is still going to continue to engage with us, and He expects the same in return from us. Our relationship with Him isn't predicated exclusively on getting things from Him. I've heard people use the expression "using prayer as a vending machine." You just come to God and demand what you want, He gives it, and you walk away without any commitment on your part! Well that isn't how God wants to ultimately relate to us. He is our Father and He delights not just in providing for us as any good Father would, but also in remaining in communion with us.

While we may be singularly concentrated on getting our specific answers for our individual concerns, God is even more concerned about growing us spiritually, developing our character and conforming us more into the image of Christ. This is especially true if in looking in our hearts, it is obvious to Him that we will not be faithful to Him once we receive our answer.

What is interesting about this is that while we may be convinced we will not forget and betray God once we get our desires, the truth is that our own hearts are desperately wicked and deceptive so that we lie to ourselves and don't even always know this is what we are capable of. Remember Jesus and Peter at the last supper? Peter was convinced that He would never betray Jesus and was vehement that it would never happen (Matthew 26:35). It was truly *not* his intent to deny Jesus. Yet he did. Three different times. And it wasn't till the cock crowed that he even connected the dots and found himself caught in his own deception (John 18:15-27). He was devastated and disappointed but obviously Jesus knew more than he Peter did. God knows us more than we know our own selves. Selah!

Our Father is also more concerned about the growth and progress of His Kingdom on Earth first, and not our necessarily our needs first (see Matt.6:31-33). In the Lord's prayer, we are to ask for His Kingdom to come first before we even ask for our daily bread, which seems a little harsh especially if you are really and truly hungry and in need. This then shows that since the Kingdom is of such significance to God, when we are pleading our case with Him for our individual needs, we must be willing to align the manifestation of our personal need with the furthering of the Kingdom.

## INTROSPECTION

In seeking the Will of God regarding a specific situation we are praying for, it is incumbent on us to search our own hearts with the Holy Spirit's help, regarding the why for our ask. This is called *introspection*. (Introspection also means self-examination and reflection.) David was not afraid to ask for the Lord to search his heart and his will. He was willing to be honest with himself and acknowledge if he could potentially be out of line. The following verses help us analyze the motivations behind our requests:

> Search me, O God, and know my heart: try me, and know my thoughts: And see if there be any wicked way in me, and lead me in the way everlasting. (Psalm 139:23-24, KJV).

As we are relying on the Holy Spirit and searching the Word of God, the Lord will help us identify where we could be believing, asking or conducting ourselves amiss.

> For the word of God is alive and active. Sharper than any double-edged sword, it penetrates even to dividing soul and spirit, joints and marrow; it judges the thoughts and attitudes of the heart. Nothing in all creation is hidden from God's sight. Everything is uncovered and laid bare before the eyes of him to whom we must give account. (Hebrews 4:12-13, NIV).

The Bible says David was a man after God's own heart. I believe he got this nickname because he cared deeply about what God had to say about everything in his life and this practice gave him the distinct honor of never having to lose a war (give me some that please!) David was instrumental in expanding the Kingdom of Israel by acquiring territories through warfare, even as we are also called to expand God's spiritual Kingdom today by winning souls and fighting back the gates of Hell.

David well understood the searching nature of God and gave his son Solomon this advice:

> "And you, my son Solomon, acknowledge the God of your father, and serve him with wholehearted devotion and with a willing mind, for the LORD searches every heart and understands every desire and every thought. If you seek him, he will be found by you; but if you forsake him, he will reject you forever. (1 Chronicles 28:9, NIV).

The King James Version puts it this way: "He understands the imaginations of your thoughts."

Did you know there are imaginations, assumptions, belief systems that underlie, produce, and reinforce our thoughts? If we are going to be effective prayer warriors, who understand the Word and Will of God, we have to consistently invoke the Holy Spirit to search our thoughts and separate our desires and needs from our motives. The more our motives align with the furthering of the kingdom, the more likely we are to have our desired results.

Jesus was often questioned about His origins, where He got His authority and doctrine from. An example of His response is:

> If any man desires to do His will (God's pleasure), he will know (have the needed illumination to recognize, and can tell for himself) whether the teaching is from God or whether I am speaking from Myself *and* of My own accord *and* on My own authority. He who speaks on his own authority seeks to win honor for himself. [He whose teaching originates with himself seeks his own glory.] But He Who seeks the glory *and* is eager for the honor of Him Who sent Him, He is true; and there is no unrighteousness *or* falsehood *or* deception in Him. (John 7:17-18, AMPC).

Jesus was defending Himself against the naysayers regarding where His authority, and therefore motivation, came from.

What is our motivation? Are we asking from our own finite wisdom, of our own accord, authority, and desires to honor our own selves or are we seeking to honor our Heavenly Father who sent us? Is what we are seeking in any way connected to or promoting any form of unrighteousness, falsehood or deception?

## MAKE DECISIONS ALIGNED WITH GOD'S WILL

Living a victorious Christian life overall is more than simply asking God for material things. It is partnering with God in our everyday decisions, big and small. Victorious Christian living is contingent on relying on the Holy Spirit to direct our steps:

> [6] In all thy ways acknowledge him, and he shall direct thy paths. (Prov. 3:6, KJV).

It is in our best interest to inquire of the Lord about every move we make, as opposed to after the fact, when we could very well be in damage control mode. Especially when we make major decisions, it is vital we analyze the known options in prayer by asking and seeking the Lord to give us specific signs and direction as we ask for illumination into His Will regarding His best choice for us.

David was a brilliant military strategist whose very life was on the line for several years. Every move he made could have had important ramifications, for many were his adversaries both from within Israel itself and from neighboring countries. He was on the run because the reigning King Saul became jealous of his popularity. Saul saw him as a direct threat to his kingship. God had already anointed David to replace Saul as king because his ways had so displeased the Lord. The book of 1 Samuel gives several examples of David's reliance on inquiring from the Lord on what his next steps were to be when he was on the run from King Saul.

In the example below, we see that He consulted the Lord, listened to his army as well, took their worries into consideration, and then asked God again to make sure he truly heard right the first time.

> Then they told David, Behold, the Philistines are fighting against Keilah and are robbing the threshing floors. So, David inquired of the Lord, Shall I go and attack these Philistines? And the Lord said to David, "Go, smite the Philistines and save Keilah. David's men said to him, Behold, we are afraid here in Judah. How much more, then, if we come to Keilah against the armies of the Philistines?" *Then David inquired of the Lord again.* And the Lord answered him, "Arise, go down to Keilah, for I will deliver the Philistines into your hand." So, David and his men went to Keilah and fought the Philistines with a great slaughter and brought away their cattle. So David delivered the people of Keilah. (1 Samuel 23:1-5, AMPC).

We realize that David's success in outwitting both the Philistines and King Saul for so many years and David's ultimate ascent to the throne in Saul's stead was due to his implicit reliance on knowing the Will of God, which came through the Word of the prophets and implicitly obeying whatever God told him to do.

We can learn from the life of Saul, too. Saul did the *opposite* of the very things that kept David aligned with God. King Saul went to a fortune teller instead of seeking the Will of God by inquiring the Word of God through the prophets.

Finally:

> Saul died because he was unfaithful to the LORD; he did not keep the word of the LORD and even consulted a medium for guidance, and did not inquire of the LORD. So the LORD put him to death and turned the kingdom over to David son of Jesse. (1 Chron. 10:13-14, NIV).

God considered Saul's error in insisting on being self-directed and willful so grave that Saul and his three sons were all killed so that God could promote David instead.

But if we, like David, will chase after God, inquire of Him, and then accomplish the fulfillment of His Will, we will see the manifestation of many of God's promises in our lives: safety, protection, fulfillment of His promises in our lives and for generations.

## IN CONCLUSION

In conclusion, working the Word of God and willing the will of God allows us to manifest seemingly impossible things that exist in the mind of God, but are waiting to birthed here in the earth realm. By working the Word and willing His Will, we literally superimpose a bit of Heaven here on Earth. We become fruitful and expand His kingdom even as God commanded us to do in the very beginning.

## THOUGHTS AND TIPS ON PRAYER EXECUTION

1. When we are inquiring of the Lord for His Will, our posture is one of humility.
2. When we are working the Word and or willing His Will into existence, we are superimposing a spiritual reality into the earth realm and enforcing it into existence. Typically, we

will get resistance from the enemy and we have to be more aggressive in the execution of our prayers.
3. David inquired of the Lord before making any moves, especially on the battlefield. What would that look like for you in your 21$^{st}$ century faith walk?
4. How do you plan to rely more on the Holy Spirit to help you effectively use the Word and your knowledge of God's will in your prayer life?

Check out our accompanying Prevailing Prayer Workbook/Journal at www.prayslayandreign.com for more tips.

## Prayer Points

- ❖ My Father, teach me to value your Word above all else and to grow in the knowledge of your Word. Let your Word dwell richly in me and Holy Spirit, bring it to my memory for your glory.
- ❖ Lord Jesus, I chose to receive your word as a child so I can enter and enjoy all the benefits of your Will.
- ❖ Matt. 6:10 says "Thy Kingdom come. Thy will be done on Earth as it is Heaven." Let the perfect will of God always prevail in my life in the mighty name of Jesus Christ.
- ❖ Anything in my life that is resisting my transformation by the renewing of my mind with the Word of God, let that thing die in Jesus' name.
- ❖ I declare that I conform my life and my will to the life of Christ and the will of God. Anything resisting my alignment to the Word and Will of God, let it die now in the name of Jesus Christ.
- ❖ I stand on Rom. 12:2 and decree that I will enjoy the good, acceptable and perfect will of God for my life, even as my mind is renewed and I conform to the image of Christ.
- ❖ Holy Spirit, illuminate my spiritual eyes to understand your perfect will for every area of my life.

CHAPTER 7

# CHRIST IN ME, THE HOPE OF GLORY

*"If you want that splendid power in prayer,
you must remain in loving, living, lasting,
conscious, practical, abiding union with
the Lord Jesus Christ."* C. H. Spurgeon

*Dear Lord, I come to You with an open heart.
Teach me what You want me to know and learn. I
want my heart to be like the fertile soil where the seed took
root. Amen.*

## CHRIST IN ME, THE HOPE OF GLORY

The title of this chapter comes from the passage below.

I have become its (the church's) servant by the commission God gave me to present to you *the word of God in its fullness— the mystery that has been kept hidden for ages and generations, but is now disclosed to the Lord's people.* To them God has chosen to make known among the

> Gentiles the glorious riches of this mystery, *which is Christ in you, the hope of glory.* (Col. 1:25-27, NIV)

In this excerpt, Paul tells us that the Word of God *in its fullness* is a mystery and that mystery is that Christ in us, literally, is the hope of glory. Jesus didn't just give us the gospel of redemption and set us free by His death and resurrection to make us His church and leave it at that. He also empowers us to exhibit the glory (brilliance or beauty) of God. As we continue to abide in Him and emulate Him and His works, we exhibit the works and power of God to the world. In so doing we show to the world that He is real, He is alive in us and is coming back again. This is the literal meaning of the expression "Christ in us, the hope of glory." Let's look at the Easy to Read Version of this same passage:

> [25] I became a servant of the church because God gave me a special work to do. This work helps you. *My work is to tell the complete message of God.* [26] *This message is the secret truth that was hidden since the beginning of time. It was hidden from everyone for ages, but now it has been made known to God's holy people.* [27] God decided to let his people know just how rich and glorious that truth is. *That secret truth, which is for all people, is that Christ lives in you, his people. He is our hope for glory.* (Col. 1:25-27, ERV)

This mystery doesn't have to remain a mystery. God wants us to know that when Jesus is allowed to truly live and rule in us it enables the amazing wonders and splendors of God to manifest in our lives. We ourselves get to be the highest forms of what God created us for. Christ in us allows the ultimate self-actualization to materialize.

Now let's look at who Christ is, our position in Him and ultimately, what this means for prevailing praying.

## THE SUPREMACY OF JESUS CHRIST

First of all, a revelation of the identity of Jesus Christ is critical to our success as prayer warriors who effect change on Earth. It is amazing to me that the disciples were in close contact with Jesus (learning from, traveling, and working with him) for some three years but they weren't actually clear on exactly who He was the whole time. They called him Rabbi, which meant Teacher, but their perception of Him was severely limited. We are similarly at risk of missing the full import of the meaning Christ if we are not careful to seek the Holy Spirit to peel back the layers on this topic of who Jesus is and for our spiritual understanding to progressively increase in this area. When the revelation occurs, we will have our own spiritual encounter of sorts with Jesus and all kinds of doors will swing open for us.

We know about the disciples' confusion because shortly before Jesus went to the cross, He asked His disciples what their understanding of Him was:

> When Jesus came to the region of Caesarea Philippi, he asked his disciples, "Who do people say the Son of Man is?" They replied, "Some say John the Baptist; others say Elijah; and still others, Jeremiah or one of the prophets." *"But what about you?"* he asked. *"Who do you say I am?"* Simon Peter answered, "You are the Messiah, the Son of the living God." Jesus replied, "Blessed are you, Simon son of Jonah, for this was not revealed to you by flesh and blood, but by my Father in Heaven. And I tell you that you are Peter, and on this rock, I will build my church. (Matt. 16:13-18a, NIV).

By supernatural revelation, Peter figured out who Christ was—the promised Messiah that Israel yearned for. Based on that revelation, Jesus conferred upon Peter the responsibility of being the first leader of the new church. Revelation brings spiritual power and promotion or elevation. Without the revelation of our Lord, as the Messiah or Chosen One to usher in the Kingdom, we are limited in our power to get results.

The fascinating story of the blind beggar Jesus healed illustrates the importance of latching on to the essence of who Christ is. When Jesus healed Bartimaeus, He was so impressed by his faith that he

*Prevailing Prayer*

took the time to mention the fact that his faith was the cause of his healing. Jesus was saying He personally wasn't directly responsible for the healing; the blind man's *faith based on the revelation of Jesus' identity* was really what clinched the deal. Jesus told the beggar:
"What do you want me to do for you?" Jesus asked him.
The blind man said, "Rabbi, I want to see."

> "Go," said Jesus, "*your faith has healed you.*" Immediately he received his sight and followed Jesus along the road. (Mark 10:51-52, NIV).

The King James Version puts it this way: "Receive thy sight: thy faith hath saved thee."
But where did that deeply assured faith come from? Let's retrace the story and see what Bartimaeus actually did differently:

> Then they came to Jericho. As Jesus and his disciples, together with a large crowd, were leaving the city, a blind man, Bartimaeus (which means "son of Timaeus"), was sitting by the roadside begging. When he heard that it was Jesus of Nazareth, he began to shout, "Jesus, Son of David, have mercy on me!" (Mark 10:46-47, NIV).

Bartimaeus recognized that the human Jesus walking past him was more than just the "Jesus of Nazareth" the crowd said was passing by. Something in Bartimaeus' spirit came alive and, like Peter, he recognized that Jesus was the promised Messiah who was going to usher in the Kingdom of God and deliver God's people. All the people crowding around Jesus saw Him as a good teacher, a mere man from Nazareth (his hometown) and so they referred to Jesus as such. But the beggar perceived *spiritually* who Jesus was and called out to Him by His real name: Jesus, the son of David, as we covered in Chapter 5 on the Kingdom of God. (The Scriptures foretold that the Messiah would come from David's descendants – John 7:42). This revelatory understanding of who Jesus is what boosted the blind man's faith and healed him.

Jesus isn't interested in your understanding of Him based on what your pastor, grand-mom or anyone else said. He wants to know what *you* personally have to say on this topic. So today, as you pursue a more productive and powerful prayer life and greater victory in your walk with the Lord, Jesus is posing the same question to you: "Dear Child, who do you say I am? Who do you think I am? What is your understanding of who I am I in relation to you? What does my very essence relate to your existence on Earth today?"

Not only is Jesus the Messiah, and the Son of God, as Peter said (Matthew 16:13-18a) and Jesus Himself approved of, Jesus is also God. John wrote this about Jesus:

> "In the beginning [before all time] was the Word (Christ), and the Word was with God, and the Word was God Himself. He was present originally with God. All things were made *and* came into existence through Him; and without Him was not even one thing made that has come into being... And the Word (Christ) became flesh (human, incarnate) and tabernacled (fixed His tent of flesh, lived awhile) among us; and we [actually] saw His glory (His honor, His majesty), such glory as an only begotten son receives from his father, full of grace (favor, loving-kindness), and truth." (John 1:1-3, 14, AMPC).

Jesus clearly states about Himself: "I and my Father are one" (John 10:30-33, KJV). This so incensed the Jews that they tried to stone Him for making Himself equal to God when they thought He was merely a man. Jesus also referred to Himself as the "I Am", the great name of God that God gave to Moses when sent him to confront Pharaoh, in John 8:58 (KJV). Finally, God Himself said of Jesus in the Old Testament that Jesus was God as prophesied by Isaiah:

> "For unto us a child is born, unto us a son is given: and the government shall be upon his shoulder: and *his name shall be called* Wonderful, Counsellor, *The mighty God, The everlasting Father, The Prince of Peace.* Of the increase of his government and peace there shall be no end, upon

> the throne of David, and upon his Kingdom, to order it, and to establish it with judgment and with justice from henceforth even for ever. The zeal of the LORD of hosts will perform this." (Isaiah 9:6-7, KJV).

There are many other verses that irrefutably settle this argument. Jesus is God.

Now, let's look at another example of the importance of a personal revelation of Jesus and its impact on the Believer from Thomas the disciple's personal encounter.

> But Thomas, one of the twelve, called Didymus, was not with them when Jesus came. The other disciples therefore said unto him, "We have seen the LORD". But he said unto them, Except I shall see in his hands the print of the nails, and put my finger into the print of the nails, and thrust my hand into his side, I will not believe. And after eight days again his disciples were within, and Thomas with them: then came Jesus, the doors being shut, and stood in the midst, and said, Peace be unto you. Then saith he to Thomas, "Reach hither thy finger, and behold my hands; and reach hither thy hand, and thrust it into my side: and be not faithless, but believing". And Thomas answered and said unto him, *My LORD and my God*. (John 20:24-29, KJV).

In this excerpt, we see that Thomas was willing to call Jesus Lord (or Master or Boss) like all the other disciples did but it wasn't till he saw and touched the risen Savior that the light bulb went off: Jesus wasn't just a great teacher, or a good man or a healer, He was GOD! Thomas' God! Church history teaches that in spite of his initial stubborn doubt, after this revelatory encounter with Jesus, Thomas became a mighty missionary for Jesus, traveling and living in India for years and converting many to the newly-found Christian faith. The Jesus-Messiah-God of the Bible has to become your personal God that you encounter by revelation too and you will see many supernatural things happen as you walk in that knowledge. Many of your inadequacies and limitations will melt away in His light.

As we examined Jesus' conversation with Peter about His identity in Matthew 16:13-18, Jesus explicitly says that the bedrock, or foundation, of His church is the revelation of who He is. In fact, no one can become a part of the church Jesus is building and using to advance His Kingdom until we first have a revelation that He is: the Christ, the Promised Anointed One; GOD. He is equal to God and is God Himself! Anything less than this full package runs the risk of falling operating under the spirit of the Anti-Christ. The Anti-Christ spirit seeks to diminish Christ, to at the very best, make Him a mere mortal and not equal with God. But Jesus is NOT just another good teacher or prophet or healer and He certainly isn't on the same level as Mohammed or Buddha or anyone else. Jesus is God:

> "Who is the liar? It is whoever denies that Jesus is the Christ. Such a person is the antichrist—denying the Father and the Son. No one who denies the Son has the Father; whoever acknowledges the Son has the Father also." (1 John 2:22-23, NIV).

What is the big deal about Jesus being the Messiah, the Christ, the Anointed One, and God? I highly recommend taking a moment to pause here and asking the Holy Spirit to illuminate Christ to you, and give you a fresh revelation of Jesus before even attempting to take this all in. You don't want these verses to fly over your head. You want to meditate on them and let them sink into your spirit, if indeed you want your prayers to be answered.

Here are a few of many verses that explain the *supremacy* of Jesus Christ:

> "*For in Christ all the fullness of the Deity (God) lives in bodily form*, and in Christ you have been brought to fullness. He is the head over every power and authority… And having disarmed the powers and authorities, he made a public spectacle of them, triumphing over them by the cross." (Colossians 2:9, 10, 15NIV)

And

> "Praise be to the God and Father of our Lord Jesus Christ, who has blessed us in the heavenly realms with every spiritual blessing in Christ... I pray that the eyes of your heart may be enlightened in order that you may know the hope to which he has called you, the riches of his glorious inheritance in his holy people, *and his incomparably great power for us who believe. That power is the same as the mighty strength he exerted when he raised Christ from the dead and seated him at his right hand in the heavenly realms, far above all rule and authority, power and dominion, and every name that is invoked, not only in the present age but also in the one to come.*" (Ephesians 1: 3, 18-21, NIV)

And

> "Therefore, God exalted him to the highest place and gave him *the name that is above every name*, that at the name of Jesus every knee should bow, in heaven and on Earth and under the earth, and every tongue acknowledge that Jesus Christ is Lord, to the glory of God the Father." (Philippians 2:9-10, NIV).

The italicized sections specifically refer to the omnipotence of Jesus. He is ALL-POWERFUL!

The name of Jesus is greater than anyone else's name, thereby making Jesus Christ superior to any other teacher, prophet or healer. Jesus is above all else, He is SUPREME!

From these three passages, we deduce the following amazing truths:

I. Jesus is equal to God; He is wholly God and the fullness of God lives in totality in Him.
II. God the Father has exalted and given Jesus the highest name and position anywhere. possible and every being/situation will have to concede this fact.
III. Jesus is the Head of everything, including all powers and authority.

IV. Jesus is triumphant/victorious over evil powers, and has disarmed and disgraced them.
V. I am in Christ who is all supreme and is seated above all rule, authority, power, dominion, and names.
VI. As a Believer, God has made His incomparably great power available for and to me.
VII. The fullness of God that lives in Christ also lives in me because I am in Christ.
VIII. I am blessed as a Believer with every spiritual blessing in Christ.
IX. There are many incomparable riches I get to partake in as part of the package of being in Him.

## CHRIST'S SUPREMACY AND OUR POSITION

I am getting excited just repeating these verses because there are so many major life-changing implications tied to these fundamental truths! Please do not skim over these nine summarized points of the verses we just covered. Take the time to really consider what they mean for your life because they are life-transforming.

We use Christ's supremacy and our position in Him to accomplish many exploits. We press the many advantages Christ has afforded us because all that He is and He has are effectively ours. We know His power is ours too. Christians who pray, slay, and reign have a powerful and productive prayer life because we understand Christ's supreme position as well as our place in Him:

> And Jesus came and spake unto them, saying, *"All power is given unto me in heaven and in earth. Go ye therefore, and teach all nations,* (*about my power*) *baptizing them in the name of the Father, and of the Son, and of the Holy Ghost."* (Matthew 28:18, KJV)

Even though Jesus referred to the enemy as the god of this world, He tells the disciples that even Satan's power is not a match for His Power because He is greater. That power Jesus gives us is greater than all the power of the enemy

> *Behold, I give unto you power to tread on serpents and scorpions, and over all the power of the enemy*: and nothing shall by any means hurt you. (Luke 10:19, KJV).

How do we win battles with the enemy? We are empowered to win because immediately after the revelation of Christ, Jesus tells Peter that the gates of Hell will not prevail against us because He is sharing a secret with us: the keys of the Kingdom:

> And I say also unto thee, "That thou art Peter, and upon this rock I will build my church; and *the gates of hell shall not prevail against it. And I will give unto thee the keys of the kingdom of heaven: and whatsoever thou shalt bind on Earth shall be bound in heaven: and whatsoever thou shalt loose on Earth shall be loosed in heaven.*" (Matthew 16:18-19, KJV).

What are keys? Keys figuratively speak of access or authorization as well as power and authority or control. How do we gain access to all the benefits of the kingdom of God, right here on Earth? How do we prevail in prayer and manifest the things in God's mind for us? We use the keys of the Kingdom which at a bare minimum involve binding and loosing and treading or trampling the enemy's works under our feet. Dear Friend, wouldn't you want to walk in that power too? Step into the realm where you take your God-given authority and use His Kingdom keys of binding and loosing to establish God's Word and Will for your life.

If we truly understand who Christ is, and the power He affords us, the enemy will not be able to run roughshod over us; instead, we will wield that knowledge and power to curtail the spread of Satan's power and his kingdom.

The next necessary step then, after we get a revelation of the identity of Christ and our position in Him, is warfare. This is because we immediately become dangerous to the kingdom of darkness and our enemies will try to resist us. If we understand these truths but choose not to take it to the next step in the faith fight: casting out, binding, and loosing (Matthew 16:19), we will not get sustained and regular victories either. After a while, we will become disenchanted with God because it will seem that He isn't coming through for us when we did not grasp the full information He presented to Peter (Matthew 16:13-18a).

The Church is lacking in power and victory because we recognize Christ is the Messiah and stop there. We are not individually and corporately embracing the full package Jesus prescribed for building and advancing the Kingdom of God. We don't see exercise our kingly authority to bind and loose because we don't fully grasp that our exalted place in Him as comes with the responsibility of using the keys (which give us authorization, control, and power) to enlarging and enforcing the Kingdom of God here on Earth. When we exercise this dimension of our faith practice, we manifest and unleash the royal prayer warrior we were created to be.

## THERE'S POWER IN THE NAME OF JESUS

Christians have been taught to always pray in the name of Jesus but become disappointed when our prayers don't seem to make it past our ceiling and there are seemingly no results. We often quote this verse:

> *And whatsoever ye shall ask in my name*, that will I do, that the Father may be glorified in the Son. If ye shall ask any thing in my name, I will do it. (John 14:13-14, KJV).

I admit I religiously prayed in the name of Jesus but still found my results were often few and far in between. It made me feel that maybe somehow Jesus was a liar—I know blasphemy to even have thought those things, but I will admit to this! I did have those thoughts and I did question God a lot about this. Why wasn't Jesus' name changing anything in my life I prayed for? But now that I know more about the Word of God, I find it amusing I really used to think that all I had to do is pray once in the name of Jesus and assume it was all I needed to do to get consistent results.

It is not enough to pray in the name of Jesus once in a while because it is not a magic wand we wave to get answered prayer when there are other areas of our thinking and lifestyle that are not in alignment to His Will and Word. For example, I was out of alignment when it came to persistence in prayer, and refusing to take my authority by implementing keys to the Kingdom such as binding and loosing. I was waiting for God to do everything for me, when I was required to take on a more active and participatory stance myself.

In light of Christ's supremacy and our position, the significance of the name of Jesus and the other names of God take on a whole new dimension. We use our superior position in Christ and His power to us to confront the enemy and fight back the forces of darkness. We are not as easily intimidated by the Devil and his devices because we know our Savior is stronger and He has the upper hand. We are less likely to be pushed around emotionally and spiritually by circumstances, bad news, and people the enemy uses against us because we know how to address the spiritual realm backing up the manifestation of these things in the natural.

## A Firm Foundation

> And why call ye me, Lord, Lord, and do not the things which I say? Whosoever cometh to me, and heareth my sayings, and doeth them, I will shew you to whom he is like: He is like a man which built a house, and digged deep, and laid the foundation on a rock: and when the flood arose, the stream beat vehemently upon that house, and could not shake it: for it was founded upon a rock. But he that heareth, and doeth not, is like a man that without a foundation built a house upon the earth; against which the stream did beat vehemently, and immediately it fell; and the ruin of that house was great. (Luke 6:46-49, KJV).

If we are going to pray productively and prevail, we have to dig deep into the Word of God, increase our foundational understanding of the things of God, and especially of Jesus, who is the mediator between man and God. Next, we have to practice those things we discover. There is no short cut around this if we want regular results. If we don't, as Jesus' words here make it abundantly clear, the very real risk is that the trials of life will overwhelm and cause us to collapse under the weight and strain of it all.

I submit to you, dear Reader, that many of us are involved in church activities or call ourselves Christians but haven't actually grasped the magnitude of the Jesus we are dealing with. Consequently, we are rendered incapable of being truly effective in prayer or in any other meaningful work that allows us to manifest heavenly things here on Earth. I, therefore, encourage you to seek your own personal revelation of who Jesus Christ is. Christ in me, the hope of glory (Colossians 1:27) will take on its own meaning in your life. If we don't fully grasp the essence of these truths regarding a revelation of exactly who Jesus is, His position and power and what being in Him (And He in us) means, we will not have victory, or our exploits will be limited.

In conclusion, walking in the full understanding of who Christ is and what we are in Him allows the manifestation of our purpose as dearly beloved children of God who emulate Christ in the Earth. A lifestyle of answered and effective prayer requires that we see Jesus or God for who He really is and address Him as such. Jesus is not a mere mortal, another great teacher. Jesus IS God. We can't successfully experience prevailing prayer, or slay and reign without appropriating and using the power Jesus freely continues to give His disciples. May God open your eyes, dear reader, to the unfathomable mystery of who our God and Savior is, and may the application of that revelation propel you to a prolific productive prayer life in Jesus' name.

## THOUGHTS AND TIPS ON PRAYER EXECUTION:

1. What does the hope of glory look like in your life?
2. In your specific situation who is Jesus to you? Provider? Healer? Prince of Peace? Jehovah our Righteousness?
3. How does your posture in prayer change upon the full realization of who Christ is and your embracing of your personal position in Him?

*Prevailing Prayer*

4. If all power has been given to you, how is your prayer life going to reflect this?
5. What have you been allowing or tolerating that perhaps you should be confronting with the name of the Lord Jesus?
6. If Christ is far above everything else, what does this mean for your personal problems? How does your view of those problems change

## Prayer Points

- ❖ I pray in the mighty name of Jesus asking that you give me a fresh revelation of Jesus Christ, even as you did for Peter. Awaken my spirit to see Jesus afresh I pray.
- ❖ Father, I thank you for blessing me with every spiritual blessing in Christ. I am grateful that I have a rich and glorious inheritance in you.
- ❖ Holy Spirit, please open my eyes to grasp the relevance of specific spiritual blessings in my life you want me to be a partaker of now.
- ❖ I plead with you to show me where I am falling beneath my spiritual privileges. I tap into your pool of spiritual blessings for me and appropriate everything that is rightfully mine.
- ❖ I ask you Holy Spirit to give me grace to walk in what is rightfully mine according to your Word in Jesus' name. I command my portion, my inheritance to be manifested in my life in Jesus' mighty name.
- ❖ In the mighty name of Jesus, let my spiritual eyes be opened so I can know the purpose of my creation and walk in my destiny.
- ❖ Lord Jesus, thank you for upending everything that is contrary or adversarial to your will for my life
- ❖ Let my life align with you and let anything adversarial or contrary to what is mine through Christ be removed so I can walk in the fullness of Christ.
- ❖ Lord Jesus, I exalt you above any other name, any other situation, any other problem, fear, doubt, sickness, etc. I crown you, Lord, over everything, including my own internal

insufficiencies and I thank you for raising me up in the areas where I am weak. I come against every adverse thing in my life that doesn't line up with your will for my life. I thank you I don't have to be subject to them either.

❖ Let the same great power of the Holy Spirit that raised Christ from the dead be made available in every area of my life in Jesus' name.

❖ By the mighty name of the Lord Jesus Christ let every good thing in me that is dead or dying be resurrected.

# CHAPTER 8

# Fired Up for the Faith Fight

*"Without faith, man can do nothing with God and God can do nothing with man."* – Samuel Chadwick

*Abba Father, since faith comes by hearing, increase my hearing and understanding of your Word and then infuse your spiritual fire in me to wage a successful faith fight. In Jesus' name, Amen!*

There are two main dimensions to this chapter: understanding the underlying principles of faith itself and then understanding what it means to fight the good fight of faith. The average Christian has heard a lot about faith. Nevertheless, I will cover some faith basics and build on them to share some deeper truths about faith. We are covering this important subject because faith has a pivotal place in unleashing the Prayer Warrior Royalty within. If you rehearse these truths and implement them into your life, you will see more answered prayers.

## THE POWER THAT WORKS IN US

Without realizing it, we typically think that prayer is only about God doing something for us when in actuality, He actually puts the weight on *us* to work with Him bring our answers to manifestation.

In the fascinating encounter narrated from Mark 9:19-26, Jesus is given a particularly thorny problem that even His disciples haven't been able to figure out. A deaf and dumb spirit within a child is resisting all attempts of being cast out. Jesus' immediate response isn't quite so charitable; apparently something about unbelief just got Jesus really riled up!

> "You unbelieving generation," Jesus replied, "how long shall I stay with you? How long shall I put up with you? Bring the boy to me..." (Mark 9:19, NIV).

I guess Jesus wasn't on the list of candidates for the most congenial kid while He was in school. Anyway, let's continue with the story:

> Jesus asked the boy's father, "How long has he been like this?" "From childhood," he answered. "It has often thrown him into fire or water to kill him. *But if you can do anything, take pity on us and help us.*" "'If you can'?" said Jesus. "Everything is possible for one who believes." Immediately the boy's father exclaimed, "I do believe; help me overcome my unbelief!" (Mark 9:21-23, NIV).

The father then proceeds with his tale of woe and shifts responsibility for the resolution to Jesus in verse 22b. We do the same thing all the time: "Jesus, *if you can do something*, please have mercy and make it happen already." But apparently, Jesus doesn't take kindly to this line of reasoning and calls out the desperate dad who just wants a quick miracle already. His response is classic but often overlooked: "It's not about what I can do, it's about what you can believe. Everything is possible for the person who has faith or who believes" (Verse 23).

Thankfully, Jesus did take over the situation and delivered the child. Nevertheless, the reality is that the Lord really wants us to clear away our unbelief blockers and build up our faith levels so we can achieve the impossible in our lives, based on our own ability to believe. There has never been a shortage of God's power. He is after all, the Almighty! However, Believers are in the driver's seat when it comes to faith. Productive prayer has less to do with what God can do and everything to do with what we are willing to believe, according to the power that works in *us*:

> [20] Now unto him that is able to do exceeding abundantly above all that we ask or think, according to the power that worketh in us. (Eph. 3:20, KJV).

## What Faith Is and Isn't

We know that faith is essential to the Believer's success as a follower of Christ:

> "But without faith it is impossible to please him: for he that cometh to God must believe that He is, and that he is a rewarder of them that diligently seek him." (Hebrews 11;6 KJV).

Let's examine what faith *is* and *isn't*.

## Mental vs. Spiritual Knowledge

Faith is *not* head knowledge. Faith is not based on human wisdom or reasoning. Faith is a highly spiritual concept and for it to truly be effective, faith has to be grasped by man's spirit, not his mind.

I come from a very intellectual family and grew up in a conservative traditional denomination. I also went to some very rigorous top-ranking schools, and was trained to value critical thinking, careful reasoning, and logical conclusions. For me, in order to really grow in my faith walk, I had to go through a process of moving away from my natural tendency to think through, rationalize, and weigh the options and move towards walking and living in faith:

> "For we walk by faith, not by sight" (2 Corinthians 5:7, KJV)

And

> This Good News tells us how God makes us right in his sight. This is accomplished from start to finish by faith. As the Scriptures say, "It is through faith that a righteous person has life." (Romans 1:17, NLT)

And

> So it is clear that no one can be made right with God by trying to keep the law. For the Scriptures say, "It is through faith that a righteous person has life." (Galatians 3:11, NLT).

Everything I knew of Christianity was head knowledge and processed through the lens of intellectualism, not unlike Paul, once known as Saul of Tarsus. Paul was also very learned, having studied at the feet of some of the greatest minds of his time. He had been a hardcore Pharisee who practiced the Law in all its intricacies. He fully understood the Old Testament rules backwards and forwards. He was also a highly skilled orator, and knew how to work a church crowd if needed. Paul was able to connect with both commoners and kings and every economic class in between. We know for example, that King Agrippa was very taken in by Paul's preaching in Acts 26:28 and wanted to convert to Christianity.

Yet, as erudite as Paul was, he was still careful not to make his teachings and preaching about fancy or eloquent words. His reasoning was very simple: he wanted their faith to be solid and unshakeable:

> My message and my preaching were not with wise and persuasive words, but with a demonstration of the

> Spirit's power, so *that your faith might not rest on human wisdom, but on God's power.* (1 Corinthians 2:4-5, NIV).

## Faith Comes by Hearing

Most churches and denominations are lacking in power and the gifts of the Spirit of God. Consequently, much of the body of Christ is not as familiar with the miracle-working power of God that we read about in the Bible as a whole, but especially the Gospels and the Acts of the Apostles. Our faith grows as we hear, and as we are exposed, to God's raw power by seeing, hearing and or reading about them. We know this because the Bible tells us that "Faith comes by hearing, and hearing, the Word of God" (Romans 10:17, KJV).

A good example of this is the story of the Samaritan woman at the well in John chapter 4. She has a conversation with Jesus in which He ultimately reveals Himself to her as the Christ. She runs back to her town telling everyone:

> [29] Come, see a man, which told me all things that ever I did: is not this the Christ? (John 4:29, KJV)

The whole town follows her back to the well because they *heard* Jesus the Messiah was there and they end up having a two-day revival with Jesus as the Preacher. When it was all over the end result is:

> And many more believed because of his own word; And said unto the woman, Now we believe, not because of thy saying: *for we have heard him ourselves, and know that this is indeed the Christ, the Savior of the world.* (John 4:41-42, KJV)

Hearing about and seeing God's power in action greatly mobilizes our own personal faith to believe God for things that, under normal circumstances, might never have crossed our minds as being within the realm of possibility. It makes perfect sense then that Paul wanted his converts to have a faith that rests on God's power and not on human wisdom. Human wisdom greatly limits our ability to have a fruitful prayer life because we are trying to realize spiritual things with head (mental) knowledge, instead of a spiritual knowledge (a reservoir comprising of examples of the acts and power of God based on His Word).

If you have not experienced the raw power of God, and been exposed to signs, miracles, healings, casting out of demons, and the gifts of the Holy Spirit it may be very hard for you to wrap your mind around.

Jesus carried a heavy anointing on Him. In the Gospels, we read of encounters He had where by simply being in His presence, demons would become agitated and start manifesting:

> And they went into Capernaum; and straightway on the Sabbath day he entered into the synagogue, and taught. And they were astonished at his doctrine: for he taught them as one that had authority, and not as the scribes. And there was in their synagogue a man with an unclean spirit; and he cried out, saying, "Let us alone; what have we to do with thee, thou Jesus of Nazareth? art thou come to destroy us? I know thee who thou art, the Holy One of God". And Jesus rebuked him, saying, "Hold thy peace, and come out of him. And when the unclean spirit had torn him, and cried with a loud voice, he came out of him. *And they were all amazed, insomuch that they questioned among themselves, saying, What thing is this? What new doctrine is this? For with authority commandeth he even the unclean spirits, and they do obey him. And immediately his fame spread abroad throughout all the region round about Galilee."* (Mark 1: 21-28, KJV).

## AWE

Faith grows in part by the amazement that comes from seeing the mighty hand of God at work. Over the years, I have purposefully sought out books, videos, teachings, testimonies, crusades, healing meetings, and conferences in which God was given a chance to do mighty things. I have seen many miracles, deliverances from demonic oppression and possession, physical healing, and outpourings of the Holy Spirit. All these have only deepened my belief in the Jesus and the power of the Holy Spirit.

These supernatural encounters are not meant to simply be a spectator sport, or cause fear in the Believer. They are really meant to stir us up in faith to press into the power of God so we can do the even greater works as Jesus promised we would. But they are to be tempered with a firm understanding of the Word of God to ensure balance.

Modern day believers who want to see more power in their prayer life and faith walk should be proactive in seeking out opportunities to see God at work because it will cause a greater appetite for the same astounding touch of God.

## Abraham and Thomas

Now, let's compare and contrast Abraham with Thomas, two men who both followed and loved God, but operated from different realms when it came to faith.

We already read about Abraham's faith in chapter 6 on Working the Word, in the section that discusses focusing on the Word of God, the Ultimate Truth, as opposed to The Facts. Abraham was almost a hundred years old, so he was past the age for having children. Also, Sarah could not have children because her biological clock had long run its course. But Abraham believed God and continued in faith. And that is why he became the father of many nations. As God told him, "You will have many descendants."

Let's look at Abraham and Sarah's story of transformation from childless and old to becoming the father of many nations, but this time from another translation.

> *So people get what God promised by having faith.* This happens so that the promise can be a free gift. And if the promise is a free gift, then all of Abraham's people will get that promise. *The promise is not just for those who live under the Law of Moses. It is for all who live with faith as Abraham did.* He is the father of us all. As the Scriptures say, "I have made you a father of many nations." This is true before God, the one Abraham believed—the

God who gives life to the dead and speaks of things that don't yet exist as if they are real. *Abraham was well aware of this, but his faith in God never became weak. He never doubted that God would do what he promised. He never stopped believing. In fact, he grew stronger in his faith and just praised God. Abraham felt sure that God was able to do what he promised* (Romans 4:16-21, ERV).

This version makes it very simple, but very real. Believers receive what God promised us by having faith. God's promises aren't just for Jews but for us who have been grafted into Abraham's lineage by receiving Christ by faith. God's word to Abraham was that he would be father of many nations (vs 17). Abraham recognized and embraced God's awesome power that was able to bring this to pass, regardless of his current circumstances. So, his faith didn't weaken; it actually grew even stronger. He never stopped believing God and took it a step further by praising God *in advance* because he was sure God was fully capable and willing to do what He had said He would do.

Thoroughly believing that God will come through on His Word even gives us license praise Him in advance, though we have nothing to show for our prayers yet. True faith acts as though what is being sought is already there.

How did Abraham build that capacity for faith? Abraham had already seen God at work in countless ways in his life already. Between Genesis 12 to 15 we see Abraham growing in his faith as he continued to walk with God. God had first called him to leave Ur, took care of him in all his wonderings, and provided for him even in great famine. God made him far wealthier, despite the drought. Abraham's faith also grew when God empowered him to take on Lot's captors and free his nephew (Genesis 14:1-16). All these things happened while Abraham was still waiting on God for his promised son to be born. So, we see Abraham going from faith to faith and each situation only further strengthening and reinforcing him.

Thomas walked with Jesus for some three years, was commissioned like the other disciples, and was sent out to preach the gospel, heal the sick, and cast out demons (Matthew 10). But Thomas (John

20:24-28) could not bring himself to believe that Jesus had risen from the dead, even though the other disciples had seen Him and Jesus told them prior to the crucifixion that He would be raised from the dead. It is possible to be around great miracles and still believe out limits on what God can do. Thomas said he would NOT believe it until he touched Jesus' crucifixion wounds first.

Abraham believed without seeing. Thomas wouldn't believe until he saw (and touched). True faith, spiritual knowledge, is born in the spirit first before seeing it in the physical world. Carnal faith, or mental knowledge, needs to see things first before it can believe that God is capable of making it happen. This is what I meant at the beginning of this chapter about head knowledge versus spiritual knowledge. It's okay to start out as a babe in Christ like this, but God expects us to mature in our faith and become capable of conceptualizing *intangible* results in our *tangible* world. In the long run, God can't honor prayers that come from a place of unbelief. He expects us to grow in faith.

## SEEING ISN'T BELIEVING BUT BELIEVING IS SEEING

From what we have read so far in this chapter and seen in the examples of Thomas and Abraham, it is apparent that faith is a spiritual exercise that has everything to do with implicitly knowing and accepting as reality what we are praying and believing, even before it materializes or manifests in the earth realm. It is undergirded by an embracing of God's word:

> Now faith is the assurance (the confirmation, the title deed) of the things [we] hope for, being the proof of things [we] do not see *and* the conviction of their reality [faith perceiving as real fact what is not revealed to the senses]. (Hebrews 11:1, AMPC).

Another version of this same verse puts it this way:

> Now faith is the substance of things hoped for, the evidence of things not seen. (Heb. 11:1, KJV).

We are required to have a vibrant spiritual faith that actively believes from our very core in the existence of God, His omnipotence, and His willingness to bring to pass what we ask. If we don't believe that we will be rewarded with answers to our prayers, we are significantly more likely to give up after a while. (After all, no one in their right mind likes to work at anything simply for the heck of it, with no recompense attached to the effort.)

There is a simple yet profound mindset approach to boosting our system of believing for manifestation. It's called visualization. While it may sound "New-Agey", this is very much a biblical principle. In Genesis chapter 15:1-6, we see that Abraham had become discouraged because his quest for a son hadn't materialized yet. He wasn't even impressed when God told him he would be His protection and prize ("I am your shield and exceedingly great reward" (Genesis 15:1, KJV) So God had to help his friend and took him outside to help him visualize his future:

> He took him outside and said, "Look up at the sky and count the stars—if indeed you can count them." Then he said to him, "So shall your offspring be." Abraham believed the LORD, and credited it to him as righteousness. (Genesis 15:5-6, NIV).

I believe this visual representation of his lineage is the picture Abraham rehearsed in his mind and that kept him on course until he got to see the reality of what he believed some twenty plus years later. Abraham *visualized* and *kept visualizing* having descendants as numerous as the stars and Isaac was finally born against all odds. God was so impressed by Abraham's belief in His ability to deliver what had been promised that "it was counted unto him for righteousness" (Romans 4:3, KJV). God called Abraham righteous not because of what he physically *did* but because he was willing to believe. Let's not forget that the Ten Commandments didn't even arrive for another 400 years after God called Abraham righteous.

Even Jesus had to do something similar. He had a tough road ahead of Him that mandated going through a terrible death at Calvary to get to His crown (resurrection and being elevated to becoming God.) But Jesus *visualized* or set the picture of the joy of obtaining the prize before Him as the motivator to keep Him going against the odds. Let's look at the same verse in two different translations:

> Fixing our eyes on Jesus, the pioneer and perfecter of faith. *For the joy set before him* he endured the cross, scorning its shame, and sat down at the right hand of the throne of God. Consider him who endured such opposition from sinners, so that you will not grow weary and lose heart. (Heb. 12:2, NIV)

And

> Looking away [from all that will distract] to Jesus, who is the Leader *and* the Source of our faith [giving the first incentive for our belief] and is also its Finisher [bringing it to maturity and perfection]. He, for the joy [of obtaining the prize] that was set before Him, endured the cross, despising *and* ignoring the shame, and is now seated at the right hand of the throne of God. (Hebrews 12:2, AMPC).

When I was separated from my husband and ambivalent about ever being reconciled, my aunt taught me this concept. She encouraged me to pray for guidance from the Lord for His perfect Will to be done in my life. Then she specifically encouraged me to ask the Lord to give me a picture of what our future would look like in that perfect Will so I could then also align myself with that picture. And so, I prayed. And prayed some more. Eventually, He gave me that picture. It was a picture I could never have conjured up by myself because I was simply so jaded and checked out I couldn't possibly see that within the realm of reality I had left behind. But God worked on my heart and through prayer, with my spiritual eyes I saw Stan, the kids, and myself in a family picture that looked like a postcard. We were at the beach on what looked like a family vacation, with the beautiful pearly white sands, gentle waves of the clean ocean and all four of us holding hands, strolling in that bucolic setting. We were surrounded by true joy and the spirit of peace.

With that picture now in my spirit, I started praying for manifestation and signs for the timing for us to reconcile and for me to move back. In God' time, He has continued to perfect that which concerns all of us in our family, to the glory of His name—not Rosetta or Stan's! Even now, when things seem a little hard and my wimpy self is feeling down and ready to give up, I pull up that mental image God gave me. And I re-affirm His promises to me. I then find strength entering me to contend for what I know is rightfully mine and soon enough, all the negativity evaporates.

We now know that believing is seeing. We see in our spirits first what we are promised. We get evidence of what we are believing for and as we maintain a healthy memory by rehearsing or fixing our spiritual eyes on that picture, continuing in prayer, and accompanying action, we get our promised results. Dear Friend, what are you praying for that could be boosted into reality by your visualization?

## THE GOD-KIND OF FAITH

Since we know from Hebrews 11:6 that it is impossible to please God without faith, let us look at examples of faith that Jesus referenced, either by modeling Himself or commending others because their faith delighted Him.

One of the more remarkable stories about Jesus refers to Him rebuking a fig tree because it didn't provide food for Him when He was hungry. Jesus was en route to Jerusalem to teach in the temple and He was disappointed to reach the leafy tree only to find out that it didn't have any fruit. Jesus essentially wished barrenness or death upon the tree in response:

> Then he said to the tree, "May no one ever eat fruit from you again." And his disciples heard him say it… Peter remembered and said to Jesus, "Rabbi, look! The fig tree you cursed has withered!" "Have faith in God," Jesus answered. (Mark 11:21-22, NIV).

*Prevailing Prayer*

That expression "have faith in God" (Verse 22) also means "have the God-kind of faith." Jesus explains that this type of faith exists in a believing heart which operates minus doubt and focuses on what the requestor *literally says out loud*. Jesus spoke out loud and so His disciples heard Him.

> And Jesus answering saith unto them, Have faith in God. For verily I say unto you, that whosoever shall say unto this mountain, be thou removed, and be thou cast into the sea; and shall not doubt in his heart, but shall believe that those things which he saith shall come to pass; he shall have whatsoever he saith. "Therefore, I say unto you, what things soever ye desire, when ye pray, believe that ye receive them, and ye shall have them." (Mark 11:22-24, KJV).

This is a very important distinction lost on many people. The God-kind of faith isn't asking as much as it is believing in the heart (your spirit man) and then declaring or confessing what is believed. Like the Royalty we were created to be and are, we are decreeing for that thing to be established. It is superimposing words that are spirit from the spirit realm and calling them into existence in the natural world.

Likewise, God didn't ask anyone for permission to create the world, but simply, *said out loud* what He wanted to do and then made it happen. We are called as Believers to walk in that God-kind of faith and make ours the things we ask for in prayer by speaking out, decreeing and/or confessing what we are believing to see manifest.

Therefore, prevailing prayer isn't just asking God to grant our requests. It is taking it a step further and aligning our words with His Word and speaking out loud our desired results in prayer and confession. This is the same pattern by which men come to salvation: we believe in our hearts that Jesus is Lord and then we confess with our lips and then we are saved:

For it is with your heart that you believe and are justified, and it is with your mouth that you profess your faith and are saved. As Scripture says, "Anyone who believes in him will never be put to shame." (Romans 10:10-11, NIV).

We will not be disappointed, or put to shame, in our prayer lives if we will believe in our hearts what we are asking for, make a positive confession out loud regarding what we are praying for, and we will see it come to pass.

## OUTSIDE YOUR COMFORT ZONE

An aspect of faith in a productive prayer life is evidenced by focus, persistence, and an overwhelming compulsion to step outside of one's comfort zone in order to see results.

For example, in the story about Bartimaeus the blind beggar, he asked what the ruckus was about, learned Jesus was in his vicinity, and proceeded to get Jesus' attention for his condition. He wasn't concerned about the needs of the others in the crowd surrounding Jesus; he was desperate for his own difficult circumstances to end. So he cried out repeatedly, in spite of the fact he was being told to shut up by the crowd surrounding Jesus:

> Then they came to Jericho. As Jesus and his disciples, together with a large crowd, were leaving the city, a blind man, Bartimaeus (which means "son of Timaeus"), was sitting by the roadside begging. *When he heard it was Jesus of Nazareth, he began to shout,* "Jesus, Son of David, have mercy on me!" Many rebuked him and told him to be quiet, *but he shouted all the more,* "Son of David, have mercy on me!" Jesus stopped and said, "Call him." So, they called to the blind man, "Cheer up! On your feet! He's calling you." Throwing his cloak aside, he jumped to his feet and came to Jesus. "What do you want me to do for you?" Jesus asked him. The blind man said, "Rabbi, I want to see." "Go," said Jesus, *"your faith has healed you."* Immediately he received his sight and followed Jesus along the road. (Mark 10:46-52, NIV).

I am sure there were many other people in the crowd who were also looking for something from Jesus, just as the woman with the issue of blood (Luke 8:43-48) in another story had her own needs that caused her to edge her way in to touch Jesus' garment. But the beggar was on his own agenda and wasn't about to worry about anyone else's.

Bartimaeus' intense focus on getting his sight, his persistence in crying out for Jesus' attention, and willingness to do whatever it took to get there paid off for him, as it has for countless Christians over the years. Think about it. The only tool he had to get Jesus' attention was his voice. Since he was blind, and didn't have a guide, there was zero chance of him getting access to Jesus. Besides, there was a throng of people around Jesus. So Bartimaeus used the one thing he had: his voice. He focused by ignoring all the naysayers, the people who thought he was too loud, disruptive, or unworthy of Jesus' attention. In fact, he cried out all the more as he was being shushed until his voice carried straight into Jesus' eardrums. Jesus was on His way somewhere, but the blind beggar interrupted Him, broke His stride, and made Jesus stand still for Him. He gave the blind beggar the attention he was seeking and asked Him what he wanted.

There's a place of desperation in needing answered prayer that will make you singularly concentrate on your end result and nothing else will matter. It will make you go outside of your comfort zone and regularly scheduled activities because you believe you are worthy in your own right of God's special attention. That type of demonstrated faith moves God's hand on our behalf and this explains why Jesus said:

> [6] Blessed are they which do hunger and thirst after righteousness: for they shall be filled. (Matt. 5:6, KJV).

Dear Reader, may the Lord increase your hunger and fill you to overflow as you draw near to Him.

## THE ROMAN CENTURION

Another character whose interaction with Jesus and demonstration of faith was worth scrutinizing is the Roman Centurion:

> And when Jesus was entered into Capernaum, there came unto him a centurion, beseeching him, and saying, "Lord, my servant lieth at home sick of the palsy, grievously tormented". And Jesus saith unto him, "I will come and heal him." The centurion answered and said, "Lord, I am not worthy that thou shouldest come under my roof: but speak the word only, and my servant shall be healed. For I am a man under authority, having soldiers under me:" and I say to this man, Go, and he goeth; and to another, Come, and he cometh; and to my servant, Do this, and he doeth it. When Jesus heard it, he marveled, and said to them that followed, *Verily I say unto you, I have not found so great faith, no, not in Israel.* And Jesus said unto the centurion, "Go thy way; and *as thou hast believed, so be it done unto thee."* And his servant was healed in the selfsame hour. (Matthew 8:5-10, 13, KJV).

This guy's faith in this story was highly commended by Jesus because he had a firm grasp of authority and understood the principle of applying the power in the spoken Word to his situation. The centurion wasn't of the Jewish faith but he understood that Jesus, like Adam, had been given dominion in the earth realm to subdue evil things like sickness. He also recognized that Jesus didn't have to break a sweat or in order to get the desired results. He had his own soldiers who reported to him and knew that as the designated "ruler" over his minions, he could command them. To him, Jesus was even more capable of doing the same things.

The centurion was *assured* of Jesus' power and ability. He recognized that Jesus in the spirit realm used a similar concept to get things done and so he recommended Jesus do what hadn't actually crossed Jesus mind yet in this particular situation: "Just speak the Word, Lord and my servant shall be healed." Imagine that: a pagan soldier telling Jesus what to do! But Jesus wasn't offended by the

Roman centurion's suggestion; He was impressed with the guy's reasoning and negotiation skills, called it "great faith". Jesus commended the gentile centurion over His fellow Jews, for being unrivaled in his grasp of faith. I especially like Jesus' closing statement to the Roman Centurion: "*Go! Let it be done just as you believed it would*" (Matthew 8:13, NIV).

What have you in your heart of hearts believed? Are you *assured* of your God's abilities? Are you confident that same power resides in you and that Satan and his minions have to give way to you if you walk in that authority? Speak the Word. Decree a thing and let it be established for you even according to the Word of God. Your beliefs and assurance are a huge part of your mindset.

As explained, this book, "Prevailing Prayer: Unleash the Royal Warrior Within" is only one part of the Pray, Slay, and Reign series which delves into Christian Mindset and Manifestation Coaching because this is where we win and lose most of our battles. The centurion's mindset forms part of a posture that is conducive for prevailing prayer. This posture has both mental and spiritual components which when practiced facilitate greater responses to prayer requests. It comes more from growing in your revelation of your Lord, Savior and God, as well as from being around others who walk in it than simply reading about it. Thanks to what we know about the things Jesus said about faith from the examples above, we also know how our individual faith-level plays a major part in prevailing prayer.

## REPEATING PRAYERS VS. VAIN REPETITION

Another misconception I grew up being taught and have since heard many times as an adult, even from Born-Again pastors comes from the line of thinking that essentially assumes that to keep asking for the same thing from God showed a lack of faith and that this is vain repetition which the Lord cautioned believers against:

> But when ye pray, use not vain repetitions, as the heathen do: for they think that they shall be heard for their much speaking. Be not ye therefore like unto them: for

your Father knoweth what things ye have need of, before ye ask him. (Matthew 6:7-8, KJV).

Consequently, I would pray once or twice about whatever my need was and then confidently think that since my Father knew my request before I even asked, and since it was unbelief to keep asking, I could sign out on that topic and wait to see God do His thing in His own time. Now, I am not saying prayers won't ever be answered in this way, but after years of getting marginal results at best, I truly started thinking God was letting me down. In true Rosetta fashion, I first blamed Him (this prayer thing doesn't work! I am wasting my time) and then started questioning if *maybe* I was the one at fault. As if our perfect God could ever be the one at fault!

I kept asking for the Holy Spirit to bring me more revelation about answered prayer. Then I realized that vain repetitions have more to do with canned, formulaic prayer requests, done more as an outward show to check off that we have been obedient than truly having a vibrant relationship based on frequent dialogue with the Father and guidance from the Holy Spirit on what to pray and say. If you are simply reciting your prayer, learned from memory without connecting the meaning of the words to your present circumstances, you are probably using vain repetitions.

Repetitive prayers are what we do when we pray based out of a sense of tradition but without the fire and the fresh breath of the Holy Spirit leading our thoughts and guiding our lips. Vain means futile or useless, inoperative or ineffective because they are devoid of any fresh inspiration of the Holy Spirit and don't move the hand of God. Vain repetitions are wishful thinking prayers, which aren't prayers at all. They have everything to do with saying the same words like "hoping" and asking if it's God's Will as opposed to standing in faith on the Word of God, rehearsing, and confessing the Word of God and consulting the Holy Spirit for His input. Vain repetitions also involve simply articulating our feelings and fears and troubles, instead of the prescribed solution in the Word.

If we are not led by the Holy Spirit in our prayers and insist on going off a script, how will we cooperate with Him even as He searches the mind of God and prays through us? How will we know what He needs right here and now? Let me give you an example.

Coming into the month of April, while leading my prayer group, I felt led by God to pre-emptively pray against costly accidents, mistakes, and any other attacks of the enemy to trip us up with unanticipated expenses that often had a way of setting us back and off-budget. So, I obeyed and we canceled every plan of the enemy, commanding all the elements, sun, moon, stars, wind to cooperate with us according to Psalm 141:5-7. About ten days later, on a Sunday, I had to use my husband's massive pick-up work truck to church, as I had left my car at our office over an hour away. Upon my return, as I was backing up into my driveway, I realized I hadn't parked as far back into the driveway as he would have preferred. I was about to climb back into the cab when the Holy Spirit clearly told me to leave the car where it was. To be honest, I initially mounted a nice argument with the Lord: "Father, please let me just park this car how he likes it; I could do without him being irritated with me right now." "Don't do it," was His response.

I remember walking away from the car with some trepidation, hoping and praying I was really hearing correctly and being obedient. The next night, we had a massive ice storm which caused the huge tree next to the car to topple over. It was amazing to see the precision with which God arranged the tree to fall. If I had moved the truck further back as I had been inclined to, it would have been decimated. And if the wind had blown the tree a few inches in the other direction, our garage and house would have been destroyed. I was in complete awe of the faithfulness of God and how He directed me on what to ask for and then how He answered the request He had directed me to pray. Seeing my obedience only further reinforced my commitment to moving in sync with Him all the more. I have seen countless stories like this in my life. I am grateful to say that now I see so many prayers answered, sometimes, literally at the speed of thought!

God is not turned off by engaged, mindful prayers that are freshly worded to Him, even if the requests are ones He has heard many times before. We know this is true because we already read about the parable of the widow and the judge (Luke 18:1-8). He said nothing about not being in faith because she kept asking to be vindicated. The seeking, therefore that Jesus was referring to has everything to do with both frequency and stamina. Our insistence on persistence in our prayer points is in itself a form of faith, not a lack thereof, unless God very clearly told you He had heard you and to drop that point. If the latter is the case, then, by all means, thank and praise Him and let it go. If not, continue thanking, praising, and making your request known to God. God is not obligated to show up in a prayer lifestyle that is characterized by irregularly showing up in His presence, flinging up prayers to Heaven once or twice, disappearing off the radar, having no communication with Him, and then expecting Him to show up with our answer.

Once I realized the value of persisting and focusing on the prayer topic in faith, I then had to overcome my personal weakness—that wondering, forgetful mind. I had to ask the Holy Spirit to show me my own way of escape, something tailor-made specifically for me to have success in this area. And He did. He showed me how to make prayer memos. "Duh! Anyone knows that" you might say. And you are right. But sometimes there is a big gap between *knowing to do something* and actually *doing it*. I knew about prayer journals. I knew about to-do lists and checking them off. I was simply unable to implement them. I was constantly chasing my own tail and never seemingly getting ahead.

The Lord led me to an online prayer journal that allowed me to capture my requests, set reminders, and the program would automatically email me reminders on what I said I wanted to pray about. I learned to start voicing and recording my thoughts, requests, and confessions on my phone. The Holy Spirit taught me how to make my case in prayer to the Father, complete with the verses that supported the Word and Will of God for my life and then record them. I would play those prayers back and use them as a springboard for productive prayer sessions on my longer drives and commute to work. In due season, watered by a more consistent prayer life, I started seeing the seeds I was planting start to germinate and bear fruit in my life. Truly, the Holy Spirit is our Helper and nothing is too hard for us if we will engage His assistance, instead of trying to do it all on our own.

## Fight the Good Fight of Faith

The Royal Prayer Warrior is a fighter. As cliched as this may sound, we are soldiers in the army of the Lord. Our Father is the King and He is also our Commander-In-Chief. He assures us that the battles we fight are His:

> Ye shall not fear them: *for the Lord your God he shall fight for you.* (Deut. 3:22, KJV)

Our success in fighting hinges in part upon an engaged loving relationship with our Father as this verse below succinctly expresses:

> One man of you shall chase a thousand: *for the Lord your God, he it is that fighteth for you, as he hath promised you.* Take good heed therefore unto yourselves, that ye love the Lord your God. (Josh. 23:10-11, KJV)

In God's eyes we are meant to be skilled warriors, just like David. It is God who equips and trains us to fight:

> Blessed be the Lord my strength which teacheth my hands to war, and my fingers to fight. (Psalm 144:1, KJV).

Not only does God train us, He gives us super-human strength to overcome our supernatural enemies. Way before action movies were made in which the good guys battle and ultimately triumph over the bad guys, we Believers, were ordained to be the true super-heroes:

> [30] For by thee I have run through a troop: by my God have I leaped over a wall… [35] He teacheth my hands to war; so that a bow of steel is broken by mine arms… [40] For thou hast girded me with strength to battle: them

> that rose up against me hast thou subdued under me. (2 Sam. 22:30, 35, 40, KJV)

and

> Thou shalt tread upon the lion and adder: the young lion and the dragon shalt thou trample under feet. (Psalm 91:13, KJV)

Royal Prayer Warriors see themselves as the skilled, supernaturally endowed and powerful fighters who win the good fight of faith. We are able to run through multitudes of enemy armies, slicing through them like a hot knife in butter. Before Hollywood showed us ninjas jumping over high walls, we were given the power to do so by our Father! We are ripped with spiritual muscles so strong that we demolish whatever weapons they are using against use including bows of steel and destroy all kinds of evil beasts fighting against us, just as we see in those computer-generated images in our modern-day fight scenes in movies like <u>The Lion, Witch and the Wardrobe</u>, and countless others.

As we already learned in chapter 4 God's Purpose for Creating Man, we humans are the only authorized agents allowed to operate on earth and so God's agenda has to work through our physical bodies. In cooperating with Him in prayer, He uses us as tools to accomplish His Will on Earth:

> [20] Thou art my battle axe and weapons of war: for with thee will I break in pieces the nations, and with thee will I destroy kingdoms. (Jer. 51:20, KJV)

and

> [5] Through thee will we push down our enemies: through thy name will we tread them under that rise up against us. (Psalm 44:5, KJV).

Using Prevailing Prayer principles and practices, we allow ourselves to be the Almighty's tomahawk or battle axe and together we push down our enemies so that their gates do not prevail over the Kingdom of God.

What an awesome time it is to be in the Kingdom, especially in these latter days! Dear Reader, I pray you rise up to the challenge of the training the Lord requires for us to be in tip top shape for His use. Let us rise up, therefore and fight the good fight of faith for our victory is already assured! Amen.

## In Conclusion

Applying these principles on faith still work today. Taking our rightful place in the army of the Lord and fighting the good fight of faith will create all kinds of disasters for our enemies and bring us untold victories and joys. Jesus wants to hear your voice. He wants to see your demonstrated faith, for faith without works is dead. If you, by faith, will perceive something pertinent about the Savior that is applicable to your request, if you will be undeterred, and keep calling out to Him, and if you will be willing to take some risks because you want your answer so badly, these principles will work for you too. Fire up your spirit man with these faith principles and fight for your answers. You will be blessed.

## Thoughts and Tips on Prayer Execution

1. How do you move personally your faith from head knowledge to an assurance in your spirit?
2. Think back over your prayer life. Can you think of a time when you believe you impressed Jesus with your faith level and saw your answer come to pass?
3. "Have the God-Kind of faith", Jesus said. Identify an area where you need to speak to certain things and command them to line up with God, as opposed to you begging God to do something for you.
4. When was the last time you reasoned with God in prayer to do something one way versus His proposed way? Do you know that He does encourage us to plead our case and to reason with Him?

## Prayer Points

- Holy Spirit, take me from head knowledge faith to spiritually conceived faith I pray in Jesus' name.
- Father, increase my faith capacity I pray.
- Holy spirit, touch my mind and my mindset even as I bring it in to alignment with you.
- Lord, I need to see you as All-Powerful and more than capable of exceeding what I could even ask or imagine. Let the ability to be assured of your omnipotence come up on me now in the name of Jesus Christ.
- In Jesus' name, I speak to every unbelief in my heart. Lord, expose my unbelief and give me grace to replace it with greater faith.
- Hear my cry, o Lord, attend unto my earnest prayer. Holy Spirit, partner with me and show me how to command the Father's attention to my prayers, even as the blind beggar got Jesus' attention.

# CHAPTER 9

# ENTER THE DRAGON, YOUR ADVERSARY

*"No one is a firmer believer in the power of prayer than the Devil; not that he practices it, but he suffers from it."* – Guy H. King

*Father, I ask for the right perspective and balance in this important area. I pray for discernment, soberness and a watchful spirit at all times. Increase my reliance on and obedience to you so I am not outwitted by the enemy. I choose to resist the Devil and I know he will flee from me. In Jesus' mighty name, Amen.*

I like martial arts movies like "Crouching Tiger, Hidden Dragon". If you are a child of God, you were essentially born into a royal family or house of ninjas or warriors. We call ourselves Warriors of the Cross. This royal warrior status is in your DNA. It is a part of your heritage and indelibly stamped in your identity, whether you will rise up and get trained or not. You, we, are the good guys. You are responsible for fighting to protect your family. Your family has spies watching the boundaries of the camp, is training for battle, and even has spies in the enemy camp.

Across town, are your family's sworn archenemies. Call them The Den of Thieves. They are always looking for an opportunity to eliminate you and your family. It's an on-going feud that stretches back to Genesis:

> And I will put enmity between you and the woman, and between your offspring and hers; he will crush your head, and you will strike his heel." (Genesis 3:15, NIV).

But somehow, you decide you don't want to be bothered. You know your enemy exists and is out to get you, but you refuse to acknowledge their existence or their intention to ultimately annihilate you. Or, you marginally recognize them as your sworn enemies, but you refuse to fight them. You are too sophisticated for that barbaric, old-fashioned stuff! You may even decide to cozy up a little closer to them, like Lot did when he decided to leave the safety of the protection of his prayer warrior uncle, and moved closer to Sodom (Genesis 19). You ignore the fact that the enmity is never going to end, at least not from their side!

Then the day comes when your enemy does somehow manage to infiltrate your fortified camp! Now you and your family are under major attack. The enemy comes with gangs of relatives, complete with their long shiny swords sizzling in the sun and slicing through the air as they expertly demolish everything you care about.

Since you couldn't be bothered to recognize your enemy for the real threat he was, you barely made any effort to prepare yourself. You pull out your rusty, dull saber but your shoulder and arm muscles are out of shape. You are too weak to swing it: boy, those warriors in the movies sure made it look easy when they tirelessly pushed back against attacks but you can't keep up with your relentless enemy.

Since you haven't been deliberate about studying the Word, the sword of the spirit (Ephesians 6:17), you barely know it! You have no knowledge of the Words that can be to throw back at your adversaries, or the shield of faith to withstand the enemies' fiery darts!

So here you are, ill-equipped for this crisis, getting badly beaten and then, having the nerve to blame God for *your* negligence because you have lost something valuable or your life is in ruins. Also, you weren't there for your family. They needed you to fight beside them!

This horrible scene ends with much bloodshed, destruction, and defeat for the Believer. Unfortunately, this is the sorry state of many a weak and spiritually unprepared Christian, either in the midst of, recovering from, or possibly heading toward an encounter with the activities of the Prince of this World, and his Den of Thieves who are out to steal, kill, and destroy (John 10:10).

We are being dangerously naïve if we think that if we ignore our adversary, then he will by default, ignore us as well. In Matthew 16:18 Jesus makes it plain to the disciples that the gates of Hell will not prevail against His true church which is built upon the revelation of Himself.

> And I tell you that you are Peter, and on this rock I will build my church, and the gates of Hades will not overcome it. (Matthew 16:18, NIV).

This sentence strongly anticipates impending satanic warfare against Believers which happens both corporately and individually. If Jesus recognized we would be attacked, then we need to stand in agreement with Him and be prepared to counteract those attacks. Pretending there is no enemy, or that he doesn't attempt to attack us or advance his own nefarious kingdom certainly does us Believers no favors.

Jesus assures us that we are already victorious against whatever onslaught of evil the enemy may try to bring our way. We are already destined to win! At the very least we need to neutralize his activities and then graduate on to being on the offense, instead of always waiting until we are picked on to rise up and fight back.

My treatment of this topic in this book is hardly exhaustive or extensive and is only meant to serve as an introduction. Book II in the PRAY, SLAY & REIGN series will cover SLAYING much more rigorously, as will additional training material found on my website.

*Enter the Dragon, Your Adversary*

## COGNITIVE DISSONANCE

It's been said that after getting Adam and Eve to give up their dominion, Satan's next greatest feat was successfully convincing the average "educated" person of his non-existence. No surprise there, the Devil's primary job is to blind the minds of men, including Christians:

> But if our gospel be hidden, it is hidden to them that are lost: In whom the god of this world hath blinded the minds of them which believe not, lest the light of the glorious gospel of Christ, who is the image of God, should shine unto them. (2 Corinthians 4:3-4, KJV).

However, not believing in the existence of Satan and the various forms he could take does not negate his actual existence. In much the same way that being unaware of traffic rules within a certain jurisdiction could land anyone some hefty fines, jail time or death. A lack of knowledge of Satan and his activities allows him to work with even less resistance, but it doesn't free us from the possibility of attacks especially when we unwittingly open ourselves up to demonic activities or traps. Neither does it absolve us of the responsibility to do the things God expects of us. Little wonder then that we are seeing such an increase in personal and corporate troubles.

## IGNORANCE AND FEAR: YOUR ENEMY'S BEST WEAPONS

Cognitive dissonance refers to a mental or spiritual inconsistency in which a person (or organization) holds contradictory beliefs that spill over into their actions or behavior. Many profess to love Jesus and vow to serve and follow Him, but when it comes to this topic, they unconsciously disagree with Him and shrink back, partly out of ignorance and partly out of fear. Both ignorance and fear are some of the greatest tools in Satan's arsenal of weapons. We must address this topic if we are to be victorious in prayer.

The Bible says "Can two walk together except they be agreed" (Amos 3:3, KJV). We can NOT walk with Jesus into victory if we don't agree with Him. By the same virtue, Jesus said that no disciple is greater or smarter than his master and so we would be wise to acknowledge His omniscience in this:

> Very truly I tell you, no servant is greater than his master, nor is a messenger greater than the one who sent him. *Now that you know these things, you will be blessed if you do them.* (John 13:16-17, NIV; emphasis added).

In this particular verse, Jesus was specifically referring to washing His disciples' feet and was admonishing them to do the same for one another. Nevertheless, the underlying message is still relevant and appropriate to this topic. You can't be a disciple of Jesus and think that something He did is somehow beneath you, or that you are smarter/more evolved/better educated and therefore, know more than He does. If you do indeed believe this then you are not a disciple after all, because no servant or disciple is ever greater than his leader or master.

Of course, we wouldn't ever actually dare to come right out and say we think we are better than Jesus is, but by our unconscious decisions and inactions we, in effect, reinforce the notion. It is ill-advised that we conveniently ignore certain truths because they are uncomfortable and hope to our desired results while operating with less than our full arsenal of knowledge. Knowledge still is power. Dwelling in willful ignorance simply opens the door for us to be taken advantage of by the same enemy we refuse to acknowledge or engage.

Some of the doors that allow direct satanic opportunity for infiltration, oppression, manipulation, etc. to introduced into people's lives include worshipping idols, bloodshed/murder (including abortion), participating in occultic practices including dabbling in astrology to foretell and govern one's decisions, consulting spiritualists or mediums to speak with the dead, getting involved in witchcraft, making evil pacts or covenants, joining secret groups like the Freemasons, etc. (see Deut. 18:9-13).

There are also Christians who do believe in the existence of the Devil, but won't educate themselves on their enemy. (How can you fight your enemy if you don't understand how he works?) Neither are they willing to engage, expose or confront him and his kingdom. They recognize his existence but that's about as far as they are willing to go. Some think that exposing the Devil and his works by talking about him will give him free publicity and so they say things like, "I don't give the Devil any glory or focus on him." Paul had something to say about this line of reasoning:

> Lest Satan should get an advantage of us: for we are not ignorant of his devices. (2 Corinthians. 2:11, KJV).

But our collective ignorance is literally killing us because we are letting our enemy get away with activities that we are responsible for stopping. Remember, we were created by God to manage and subdue this earth. We are literally law enforcement officers whose job is to beautify the earth by subduing satanic activity and we are falling asleep at the wheel.

As the end times approach, there are even more intensified satanic schemes, efforts, and activities taking place in the earth realm to keep blinding the eyes of the unsaved so they don't come to know Jesus. There are more people practicing witchcraft openly, complete with their bumper sticks and lawsuits. Others are gaining power through hexes, spells, voodoo dolls (yes, right here in America too, so please don't make it only about things that happen in Africa) There is also a concentrated effort against Believers, to keep us complacent, distracted, broke, sick, etc. and ultimately from rising up to our true potential and destiny. All while we Christians hide our heads in the sand and wonder why we never seem to get ahead.

In Isaiah 5:11-14, the prophet accurately describes our times. These are times in which the gates of Hell are expanding: "Therefore hell hath enlarged herself, and opened her mouth without measure" (verse 14a). Hell is capturing or swallowing up tens of thousands of souls daily because we "regard not the work of the Lord, neither consider the operation of His hands" (verse 12b).

> [11] Woe unto them that rise up early in the morning, that they may follow strong drink; that continue until

night, till wine inflame them!¹² And the harp, and the viol, the tabret, and pipe, and wine, are in their feasts: *but they regard not the work of the* LORD, *neither consider the operation of his hands.*¹³ *Therefore my people are gone into captivity, because they have no knowledge: and their honorable men are famished, and their multitude dried up with thirst.*¹⁴ *Therefore hell hath enlarged herself, and opened her mouth without measure: and their glory, and their multitude, and their pomp, and he that rejoiceth, shall descend into it.* (Isaiah 5:11-14, KJV).

According to this passage, we, God's people are going into captivity because we have no knowledge. What knowledge you may ask? What is the work of the Lord and the operation of God's hands referred to here? We have no knowledge of our enemy's schemes. We are lacking knowledge of our rightful inheritance as royal prayer warriors, in whose physical lives and hands God has placed His ability and power to accomplish His work on the earth in. So, Hell is gaining ground on us. The same gates of Hell Jesus said would not prevail over us if we used His keys to the Kingdom of binding and loosing are enlarging their borders because we are not doing what we are supposed to (Matthew 16:17-19).

Consequently, we are being targeted with all kinds of spiritual attacks like sickness, marriage destruction, drug addiction, and in-fighting in our churches while we sing beautiful praise songs to God. We entertain weak individual and corporate prayer lives and chase diluted doctrines that focus mostly prosperity and happiness and how God is going to come through for us, while we do nothing to partner with Him in to make it happen. But the evidence of our lack of knowledge of our enemy is all around us. All kinds of evil spirits have been loosed on the earth and we haven't confronted them. The best we seem interested in doing as the body of Christ is cozying up to the political machinery, erroneously assuming we can fight satanic onslaught through political parties at the ballot. All of this is at the expense of a prevailing prayer life when Jesus specifically said that His kingdom is NOT of this world. These are all some of the devices Paul is referring to in 2 Cor. 2:11.

As mentioned, the enemy uses fear as a great tactic against Believers. While it is true he can be a formidable enemy, the truth remains that Jesus has destroyed his works and the name and blood of Jesus still have the greatest power. We already read in chapter 7 "Christ in Me, The Hope of Glory" whose we are (Jesus') and who we are in Him (victorious). Jesus has already destroyed and disgraced Satan and his hordes. We Believers just have to enforce the work of the cross in our prayer lives.

This fear that drives many Christians to pull back from knowing and engaging the enemy is in itself unfounded. The Bible tells us that there is no fear in love:

> Herein is our love made perfect, that we may have boldness in the day of judgment: because as he is, so are we in this world. *There is no fear in love; but perfect love casteth out fear*: because fear hath torment. He that feareth is not made perfect in love. (1 John 4:17-18, KJV; emphasis added).

If we truly love Jesus and truly understand His love for us, we will not fear the Devil. We will act like Him and that is what will make us bold in the day of judgment. We will not stand before God and be embarrassed or afraid because we acted just like Jesus did and commanded us to.

There are many verses in the Bible that discuss Satan and his activities. Not all the verses refer to him by his more commonly known names like Lucifer, Devil, and Satan. He is a real spiritual being, not a figment of our imagination. He was originally a beautiful angel, the most senior ranking angel who then went rogue. He wanted to overthrow God so He could take God's place and be God. His plans were thwarted and he was cast out of Heaven to Earth and relegated to Hell instead as his final destination. His powers of persuasion are great, for it is believed that about a third of all the angels chose to follow him in rebellion against God.

> How art thou fallen from heaven, O Lucifer, son of the morning! How art thou cut down to the ground, which

> didst weaken the nations! For thou hast said in thine heart, I will ascend into heaven, I will exalt my throne above the stars of God: I will sit also upon the mount of the congregation, in the sides of the north: I will ascend above the heights of the clouds; *I will be like the most High*. Yet thou shalt be brought down to Hell, to the sides of the pit. (Isaiah.14:12-15, KJV).

And

> And there was war in heaven: Michael and his angels fought against the dragon; and the dragon fought and his angels, and prevailed not; neither was their place found any more in heaven. And the great dragon was cast out, that old serpent, called the Devil, and Satan, which deceiveth the whole world: he was cast out into the earth, and his angels were cast out with him. And I heard a loud voice saying in heaven, "Now is come salvation, and strength, and the kingdom of our God, and the power of his Christ: for the accuser of our brethren is cast down, which accused them before our God day and night." (Revelation 12:7-10, KJV).

Satan and his hordes of fallen angels were cast into the earth and are now working overtime to take as many humans as they can to Hell with them. Satan is evil personified and because of God's great love for man, he hates humans in a way that cannot be easily described. Here are a few hallmarks of his handiwork which are easily attributable to his interference in our lives.

## SOME ACTIVITIES OF THE ADVERSARY:

We 21$^{st}$ century Christians would be in a much better place of victory if we were better equipped to identify when the enemy is at work against us. Here are but a few of the hallmarks of the enemy's hand at work behind the scenes in natural situations against the people of God:

- ❖ **Satan Accuses God's Children**: He is the accuser of the brethren in Rev. 12:10. Job and Joshua were both unfairly accused by Satan. (Job 1 and Zech. 3:1)
- ❖ **Satan Resists or Opposes** God's plans and promises from coming to fruition by a variety of devices including hijacking, aborting, stealing and/or disrupting good things. (Dan. 10:12-14) The same is true of his activities toward men, especially those aligned with God.
- ❖ **Satan Prowls and Devours.** The word prowls refers to lying in wait for an opportune time to pounce, and devours connotes swallow up, drown or overwhelm (1 Peter 5:8)
- ❖ **Satan Provokes and Leads Astray:** rises up against or tempts men to go outside the will of God (1 Chron. 21:1)
- ❖ **Satan Murders, Destroys and Takes Away**: Steals, kills and destroys (John 10:10)
- ❖ **Satan Deceives and Lies**: he is devoid of the truth and therefore perverts the truth while he lies chronically lying (John 8:44). He cunningly works by blinding minds and seducing people away from the truth with his seeming beauty, worldly thoughts, and value systems and/or strongholds that are contrary to the Word of God. (2 Cor. 11:14) He thrives in anything that is shrouded in dishonesty, secrecy or takes away your personal power when uncovered
- ❖ **Satan Entices and Seduces:** Works very subtly in most instances but also can be very sudden, forceful and with much compulsion, driving people to feel the need to do something completely out of character and to do so urgently.
- ❖ **Satan is Prideful**: at his core, Satan is arrogant and everything about his nature is rooted in pride and promotion of self. Pride was his original sin, for he was beautiful and thought based on this that he could unseat God

If you are confronted by situations in which any of the above play a prominent root cause, you are most likely under some form of demonic attack, influence or manipulation. You must pray for the

Lord to open your eyes to see more clearly and to show you a way of escape, regardless of the source.

Unfortunately, many Christians even when correct in their assessment of the source of their troubles can wrongly focus on the fruits of the problem, instead of its roots. For example: if your Christian husband decides he is interested in open relationships and expresses interest in moving in that direction and you immediately focus on your personal inadequacies, maybe your flat chest as opposed to the fact that his mind being confused by the illusions of the enemy, then you are indeed focusing on the fruit not the root of the problem. Another example: If food addiction leads to obesity and you finally get weight loss surgery and finally become an "acceptable" weight only to develop an addiction to painkillers or sex or something else, you know that you only dealt with the fruit or manifestation of the problem and not the root cause that fueled the addiction in the first place. A prevailing prayer warrior will make a deliberate and careful inquiry from the Holy Spirit to truly recognize the root cause at the bottom of these spiritual problems and then deal with them in the name of the Lord Jesus, commanding them to bow to His authority, and break their hold of your life.

There is no name that is higher than the name of Jesus and so no matter what we face, whether satanic or natural, we still have to make it submit, confess and bow to the name of Jesus (Philip 2:9-11). In bowing or surrendering, they are accepting that He is superior to them and have to leave His child alone.

## THE ROLE OF DISCERNMENT

Discernment is of vital importance to the prevailing prayer warrior, and all the more so in spiritual warfare. If we don't have discernment, we will either not see the enemy right in front of us, or we will figure out something is amiss but ascribe the problem to the wrong root cause. It's hard to fight and win a war with a nebulous, nameless enemy and the precise strategy to defeat the enemy will be harder to determine. As in all situations, rely heavily on the Holy Spirit for revelation, knowledge, understanding, and insight to craft your personal plan of attack. You are, after all, a winner. It's in your DNA:

> Behold, I give you all power to trample on serpents and scorpions and nothing shall my any means harm you! (Luke 10:19).

Doubtless, some situations are man-made; not everything is the Devil's fault because we have a free will and we get to choose. Others have satanic origins, as we well know from Job's story. It is possible nevertheless, to have a man-made situation that is demonically influenced so that we see that resolution to the original problem is delayed, deepened or worsened, and even reinforced to the point where it is prolonged into further generations.

Luke, who wrote one of the gospels and the book of the Acts of the Apostles, was a medical doctor. We see that in his writings he differentiates between a sick mother and many others who had physical ailments, for example, and other illnesses or situations which were demonically caused (Luke 7:21). Jesus, the disciples and Paul dealt with both types of problems just as easily, and ultimately, so must we. This leads us to our godly call to action.

## RESPONDING TO SATANIC ACTIVITY

James 4:7-8 shows us a clear pattern for overcoming the enemy.

> ⁷ Submit yourselves, then, to God. Resist the devil, and he will flee from you. ⁸ Come near to God and he will come near to you. Wash your hands, you sinners, and purify your hearts, you double-minded.

We are to first submit ourselves to God, then resist the enemy, even as we draw nearer to God and continually cleanse our hearts and minds. As Law Enforcement Officers in the Army of the Lord, we are called to resist. Resisting involves putting up a fight, or pushing back using various weapons we will discuss below. As we do so, the Devil will flee from us. This is how we reign and gain our victories.

Our Savior Jesus is the author and the finisher of our faith (Heb. 12:2), and we must model Him (in every area of our lives) after His example. The Bible tells us there is no temptation we go through that isn't common to man, and that Jesus was tempted on all points yet is without sin (Heb. 4:15). In the retelling of his temptations after the forty-day fast, Jesus responded directly to Satan every single time with the words: "It is written." There is no more effective antidote for the child of God than the well-rehearsed and highly familiar Word of God.

Jesus shows us then that our nuanced understanding of God's Word is critical to our success at fighting the enemy. This explains why this book is so heavily infused with Scripture which I humbly ask you to carefully assimilate. It is critical to our success in recognizing the many perversions of God's Word that the enemy throws at us to entice us to fall away from God.

Jesus also shows us that Satan's attempts to derail us can come through familiar, even trusted sources, not excluding our own selves. We are still responsible for recognizing when such situations arise and deal with him appropriately. For example, when Peter tried to discourage Jesus from going to the cross, Jesus quickly recognized Satan using Peter to try to derail God's plans for His life and stopped him dead in his tracks, just as we are also supposed to.

> Jesus turned and said to Peter, "Get behind me, Satan! You are a stumbling block to me; you do not have in mind the concerns of God, but merely human concerns." (Matthew 16:23, NIV).

Unfortunately, like many of us, Eve didn't recognize the enemy speaking through the serpent in the garden. He was at the very least an acquaintance she frequently communicated with so that there wasn't anything unusual about their interaction. Likewise, the enemy can inject thoughts and feelings into our minds, which we could unsuspectingly accept as our own.

It took a while for me to recognize that I most experienced the most intense thoughts of anger, resentment, and even hostility toward my husband during special times of intimacy and loving family situations. It was all the more confounding to me because as far as I was concerned, even if there had been a prior disagreement or some other issue, we had already hashed it out and I had released unforgiveness, bitterness, and anger long ago. But right at the time when I was supposed to be enjoying these activities that brought us closer together, these negative emotional intrusions would arise. My mind would suddenly become flooded with these intense, uncalled for feelings at these particular times that I would emotionally pull back. The enemy of my soul and marriage was trying to set up more strife and division between us.

Once the Lord showed me what was happening and told me they weren't even my thoughts at all, just the enemy projecting into my mind, I started rejecting them whenever they showed up. In my mind, and sometimes out loud or under my breath, I would pull down every thought that were exalting themselves against the obedience and knowledge of God. It wasn't till I did these things that I started experiencing victory in this area and further happiness in my marriage.

## DEAL AGGRESSIVELY WITH THE DEVIL IN CHRIST'S STRENGTH

Standing in our delegated authority requires us to aggressively get the enemy out of our way when he comes with some suggestion that is contrary to God's truth. We are not to entertain them, negotiate with them or allow them to take seed in our hearts. We are to confront those suggestions for what they really are: a distraction or worse from the pit of Hell, and speak out loud to the situation.

God's Word in our believing mouths is a mighty sword that carries great power and accomplishes much. When John was given the visions in Revelations, Jesus appeared to him with a sharp two-edged sword in His mouth (Rev.1:16). That sword is the Word of God. This same theme is also explored in the Old Testament where Isaiah says:

> "Listen to me, you islands; hear this, you distant nations:
> Before I was born the LORD called me; from my mother's

womb he has spoken my name. *He made my mouth like a sharpened sword,*" (Isaiah.49:2 KJV)

Resisting the Devil in this manner is a spiritual exercise that transpires in our thoughts, and also by confession of the Word in prayer where we attack our adversary. Our fight is not in the natural, it is very much a spiritual fight and less in the natural where people are sometimes unsuspecting pawns.

Paul gives insight into Satan's kingdom and how to successfully overcome Him:

> *Finally, be strong in the Lord and in his mighty power. Put on the full armor of God, so that you can take your stand against the Devil's schemes.* For our struggle is not against flesh and blood, but against the rulers, against the authorities, against the powers of this dark world and against the spiritual forces of evil in the heavenly realms. (Ephesians 6:10-12, NIV).

We will never overcome the enemy in our own strength. This is why we have to be strong in the power of the Lord, and not in our own abilities. It's really not about us at all. It's always been all about our Jesus and His capabilities. He is the promised sacrificial Passover lamb who completely destroyed the Devil's power by defeating the spiritual death all humans must endure because of Adam and Eve's fall. We therefore overcome the enemy by the blood of Jesus. And this is why we submit ourselves to God first before we can effectively resist our enemy.

## BECOME MORE FAMILIAR WITH SATANIC ACTIVITIES SO YOU CAN CONFRONT THEM

Paul tells us that the Devil fights the people of God with all kinds of strategies, organized systems, devices, and personnel. These personnel include rulers or principalities, who are the most senior-ranking under Satan. There are both wicked spirits with great powers on this earth as well others who are in the heavenlies. All of these entities conspire and work hard to keep men separated from

God, held in bondage and servitude to their leader Satan. They also oppose, frustrate, hinder, and confuse the work of God from taking place in the earth while trying to discourage the people of God, and even get them to abort their assignment.

This is a reality that is beautifully illustrated in the Old Testament by Daniel who had been seeking the Lord with a fast for twenty-one long days. On the twenty-first day, an angel appeared to him and explained he had been dispatched with an answer from the very throne room of God in the third heavens only to be detained on his way to Earth by an evil prince in the second heavens:

> Then he continued, "Do not be afraid, Daniel. Since the first day that you set your mind to gain understanding and to humble yourself before your God, your words were heard, and I have come in response to them. *But the prince of the Persian kingdom* resisted me twenty-one days. Then Michael, one of the chief princes, came to help me, because I was detained there with the king of Persia. (Daniel 10:12; NIV).

So, picture for a moment that this is you, praying, fasting, and seeking God for an answer to a problem in your life. You have been anticipating an answer, doing everything right and you are confident the Lord will answer you. A few weeks go by. No answer. Then it stretches into months. You have long completed your fast, you continue to pray and wait on God. But you never once acknowledged or pre-emptively confronted the enemy.

Then, you start getting mad at God (or conclude it wasn't His will) because He seemingly didn't respond. The possibility is that the angel with your answer has been arrested on his way by a more powerful evil entity never crosses your mind. Your designated messenger angel is in need of divine reinforcement and your answer risks being permanently stolen by the enemy. In your world, the Devil barely exists so how would this scenario arise? You never rebuked any adverse activities of the enemy regarding the answering of your prayer to cease in Jesus' name. You therefore have not, because you asked not. (James 4:2b). But at some point, you become offended or discouraged by the wait or apparent lack of response from God and you wrongly conclude that spending all this time in this "prayer thing" isn't worth it after all. However, it wasn't God who failed you; it was your lack of knowledge and praying the right things that failed you. You therefore didn't prevail over the enemy. He, rather, prevailed over you. God says:

> "My people are destroyed for lack of knowledge: because thou hast rejected knowledge, I will also reject thee, that thou shalt be no priest to me: seeing thou hast forgotten the law of thy God, I will also forget thy children." (Hosea 4:6, KJV).

But either way, Satan is very happy. You are one more discouraged saint who is weaker and no wiser, because he barely exists in your book. You believe that being informed of and paying attention to the Devil's schemes is somehow glorifying Satan and taking our focus away from God. These are all lies cleverly planted in to the body of Christ by Satan, the Father of lies so he can have an advantage over us.

While the Bible has several references to demonic activities, Christian converts from hard-core Satanism also provide many insightful details on the kingdom of darkness and their activities. These can be a tremendous source of extra-biblical knowledge that provide more exposure into how the enemy operates and gives us prevailing prayer warriors many helpful ways to recognize and counter-act the works of the enemy.

## Pray Pro-Actively not just Reactively

Now, while we may not know all the intricacies taking place in the spirit realm for every single situation that arises in our lives, once we understand the basic ways in which our adversary operates, we have to pray pre-emptively against whatever route he chooses to come at us. This is why in Job Chapter 1, we read about Job periodically praying and offering sacrifices to God on behalf of his children to ward off any opportunities for the enemy to have an advantage over them. Christians must be mindful of pre-emptively praying against the plans and works of the Devil, canceling them from materializing in our lives in the name of Jesus.

When Jesus was teaching the disciples to pray, on His list of prayer points was "Deliver us from evil." A very critical aspect of prevailing prayers is warfare prayers. He didn't teach us to wait till we were in trouble to ask to be delivered; we are to pro-actively stop evil from overtaking or overwhelming us. Prevailing prayer isn't just reactive, working to undo the damages of the enemy. Prevailing prayer is pro-active and pre-emptive. Prevailing prayer stops the enemy's activities from ever showing up in the natural. Prevailing prayer over-rules diabolical plans and stops them from ever being implemented.

When my eyes finally opened into this particular area of prevailing prayer, it changed my life. My perspective on my problems changed. I was supposed to be implementing a regimen of prayer that included SLAYING, in addition to the foundational principles for prevailing prayer in order to really reign with Christ. Once I started seeing how my prayers changed my day, how much power my words in prayer had and the speed with which so many prayers came to fruition, I really felt compelled to share these secrets with other Christians who want more. If we have an incomplete prayer life because we remain willfully ignorant in this area, our prayers can remain unanswered or take an unnecessarily long time to be answered. The enemy is a specialist in hindering or delaying things from happening.

## WALK IN YOUR AUTHORITY, USE GOD'S POWER

Furthermore, the reality is that many prayers are not being answered because we are asking God to do things He has already equipped us to do and God is not obliged to bail us out simply because we refuse to stand on our own two feet and walk in the authority He has imparted to us.

> And Jesus came and spake unto them, saying, *All power is given unto me in heaven and in Earth. Go ye therefore,*

> *and teach all nations, (about my power)* baptizing them in the name of the Father, and of the Son, and of the Holy Ghost." (Matt. 28:18, KJV).

And

> Behold, I give unto you power to tread on serpents and scorpions, and over all the power of the enemy: and nothing shall by any means hurt you. (Luke 10:19, KJV).

Walking in the authority Jesus gave us includes commanding and ordering things, both supernatural and natural. We all have heard the story of Jesus commanding the storm on the sea to stop:

> And he arose, and *rebuked the wind*, and said unto the sea, *Peace, be still. And the wind ceased, and there was a great calm.* And he said unto them, Why are ye so fearful? how is it that ye have no faith? (Mark 4:39, KJV).

However, we rarely hear we are also supposed to *rebuke* and *speak* to the turbulence in our lives and *command or order* the evil winds blowing to go away. To rebuke means to reprimand or scold from a place of power or delegated authority, even as a parent has the rightful position to scold or correct a child. When was the last time you scolded the negative things in your life and commanded them to settle down? This is true for medical symptoms, fear, lack, depression, any and everything, if you will have the faith. It may sound impossible but it is very real. It happens all the time, and not just for Rockstar pastors, evangelists, and prophets. These are all forms of resistance required for our prevailing prayer.

One of the areas I feel strongly God wants for the modern-day Believer to grow in is this area of developing our spiritual authority in prayer. God wants us to be comfortable commanding, overthrowing, rebuking, tearing down, and planting up, just as instructed Jeremiah when He first called him:

> Then the Lord reached out his hand and touched my mouth and said to me, "*I have put my words in your*

*mouth.* See, today I appoint you over nations and kingdoms *to uproot and tear down, to destroy and overthrow, to build and to plant."* (Jeremiah 1:9-10, NIV).

Like Jeremiah, we are responsible for implementing this component of prevailing prayer in our prayer regimen.

I have seen marriages literally crumble like dominoes down a whole block and bypass the one Christian home where the wife who stood on her watch and refused to let the Devil wreck the same havoc in her family. She would pray pre-emptively against confusion, strife, misunderstandings, marriage-wrecking women, and/any other strategy the enemy could come up with. She would command her own attitude and her husband's to submit to Christ's and come against natural fleshy responses or anything else that the enemy could exploit to his advantage.

You too can command peace to come in to your situation using the mighty name of Jesus. If you will build up your spiritual faith muscles, the Lord's power will grow in you. If you will allow yourself to grow in God's strength and power, as opposed to looking at your own pitiful human limitations you will be on the path to victory and victory will come if you will stay the course.

## PUT ON YOUR ARMOR

There is no meaningful conversation about warfare without discussing the armor of God because God always presents ways of escape for whatever difficulty we may face.

> Put on the full armor of God, so that you can take your stand against the Devil's schemes. Therefore, put on the full armor of God, so that when the day of evil comes, you may be able to stand your ground, and after you have done everything, to stand. Stand firm then, with the belt of truth buckled around your waist, with the breastplate of righteousness in place, and with your feet fitted with the readiness that comes from the gospel of peace. In addition to all this, take up the shield of faith, with which you can extinguish all the flaming arrows

of the evil one. Take the helmet of salvation and the sword of the Spirit, which is the word of God. And pray in the Spirit on all occasions with all kinds of prayers and requests. With this in mind, be alert and always keep on praying for all the Lord's people. (Ephesians 6:11, 13-17, NIV).

We really don't have to be victims or casualties of the enemy's onslaught. We can prevail and win! What makes Pray, Slay & Reign a powerful and productive signature system for results-oriented prayer is the combination of truly praying in alignment with the whole counsel of God and the practice of exercising our authority to keep the enemy in check so we can reign with Christ now and in eternity. Please be on the look-out for updates on additional material specifically on this topic by signing up on my website www.prayslayandreign.com. In conclusion, let us reconsider our earlier depiction of what true prevailing prayer looks like, picking up from where we left off in chapter 2, Platform for Prevailing Prayer.

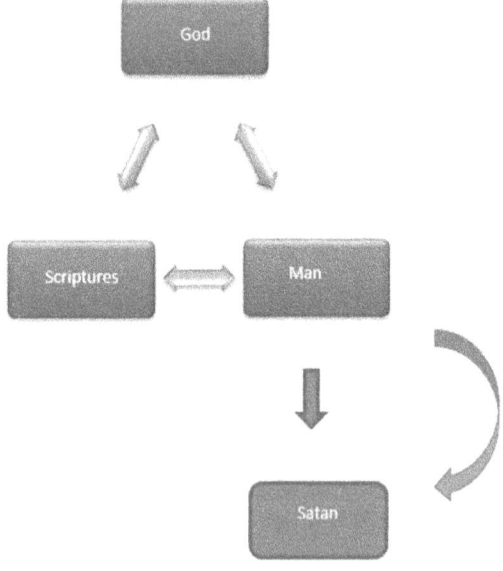

The curved arrow refers to the various means by which we keep the enemy under his rightful place, which is under our feet. We have learned that the Word of God (also known as the sword of the spirit), commanding, rebuking, casting and binding, loosing, even speaking destruction into unsatisfactory situations (remember Jesus and the fig tree) are part of the arsenal Believers use to effectively keep the enemy in check. Additionally, our other weapons of warfare include the blood of Jesus, the name of Jesus, utilizing angels to minister to us and fight on our behalf, praises to God, our positive declarations or profession, and the full armor of God.

No victorious Believer can sustain their Christian existence and reign without effective spiritual warfare involving at least some of these elements. I will deal exclusively with the SLAY part of the PRAY, SLAY & REIGN series and I will delve very deeply into some of the intricacies of Satan and his kingdom. The information about warfare, the strategies and prayer points will catapult your prayer life to the next dimension. I highly recommend signing up on our updates page as I will be sending out thought-provoking excerpts from this book. Let it suffice for you to know and practice these preliminary truths I have shared thus far about your adversary and how to overcome him.

## TIPS AND THOUGHTS

1. Have you faced a time when you felt like your adversary was prowling around, looking for a chance to pounce?
2. When was the last time you successfully resisted the Devil and he fled from you?
3. What would be the appropriate mindset and attitude needed to resist, rebuke, command, bind, and loose in Jesus' name?
4. How comfortable are you exercising your Biblical authority as a Royal Prayer Warrior?

## PRAYER POINTS

❖ In the mighty name of Jesus, I refuse to be ignorant of the wiles of the enemy.

*Prevailing Prayer*

- ❖ Holy Spirit, open my eyes to discern and recognize every deception of the enemy in my life.
- ❖ Lord, show me how to effectively walk in your power.
- ❖ I take up the mighty weapons of warfare and I pull down every mental stronghold that is making me resistant to the whole counsel of God in this area of my Christian faith.
- ❖ Let the Word of God dwell richly and abound in my heart so I can quickly and easily overcome every temptation and attack of the enemy in the mighty name of Jesus.
- ❖ Holy Spirit, you are my senior partner. I put my hands and life in your hands. Direct me I this area of my walk to grow and efficiently handle the responsibilities that come with this.
- ❖ Spirit of counsel and might, I ask that you show me how to pray proactively and pre-emptively against the enemy.
- ❖ My Heavenly Father, deliver me and my household from evil even now in the mighty name of Jesus. Let no plan of the enemy prevail against me in Jesus' mighty name I pray.

CHAPTER 10

# THE PRACTICE OF PREVAILING PRAYER

*"There is no way to learn to pray but by praying… Though a man should have all knowledge about prayer, and though he understands all mysteries about prayer, unless he prays he will never learn to pray." – Samuel Chadwick, The Path of Prayer*

*Abba, Father make me a doer of what you have taught me and not just a hearer. I pray that I will not be one of those who has itching ears and heaps on knowledge after knowledge, yet never makes any real progress. Give me the supernatural skills and abilities it takes to implement the practice of Prevailing Prayer and to go even further to develop the practice of Prevailing Prayer. Amen.*

Much of this book has been focused on the acquisition of the foundational Biblical principles that form the body of knowledge needed to equip us to enjoy a prevailing prayer lifestyle. Now we are going to pivot to the actual execution or

*Prevailing Prayer*

practice of prevailing prayer. As Royal Prayer Warriors, this is how we PRAY, SLAY AND REIGN!

The traditional prayer model most Christians are familiar with follows this general format: ACTS: Adoration, Confession (of sin), Thanksgiving and Supplication. Prevailing prayer encompasses a few more steps in its lifecycle from start to finish. I recommend starting with all four steps of ACTS and then continuing with the acronym WIDERM.

**A**doration: Praise and worship our Father.

**C**onfession: Acknowledge and Repent of all sins known and unknown.

**T**hanksgiving: Appreciate the Lord for everything, even what you want changed.

**S**upplication: Present perceived needs to Father, ask for uncovering of true need.

**W**ord: Discover relevant Word and Will of God that deals with/speaks to situation.

**I**nternalize: Meditate on that Word till faith arises.

**D**eclare: Speak and superimpose God's Word over current circumstances.

**E**xercise spiritual authority over evil agenda and operation of the enemy.

**R**epeat all or some of the above especially A, S, W, T, D, E until

**M**anifestation arrives.

Let's break-down this steps of ACTS WIDERM into more detail:

**Adoration**: Praise and worship are particularly important because they are things that God can NOT do for Himself. Our adoration must be sincere and come from a place of experience. Our praise and worship magnify God in our eyes so we are primed into an atmosphere of Praise and worship minimalizes our own selves. Our proper adoration also paves the way for expectancy, which is the breeding ground for miracles to manifest.

**Confession**: We genuinely repent and ask for forgiveness of all sins, whether by commission or omission not just for ourselves individually, but also on behalf of our families, ancestors, and nation (Nehemiah 1:6-11). We confess because sin separates us from the Lord, and confession brings us back into fellowship with Him. God assures us that if we humble ourselves He will forgive our sins (2 Chronicles 7:14).

**Thanksgiving**: Gratitude reflects an appreciative acknowledgment of God's hand in what we already do have, no matter how bad and pressing our needs are (Psalm 100, 1 Thessalonians 5:18).

**Supplication**: When we are confronted by an issue, we present that situation to the Lord for His intervention. Nevertheless, we want to ultimately avoid praying from a place of complaint and grievances. At the same time, it is possible that our perceived problems and assumed answer to them may be quite wrong-headed in God's eyes. The Bible refers to this as "asking amiss" (James 4:3). Thus, it is imperative we truly seek God's face about the root problem at stake and align ourselves correctly with His mind on the issue so we are praying in the first place for the right thing.

Supplication isn't just praying for external or physical things. It is also entails petitioning God about the condition of our own hearts so that we are in agreement with Him. This is where submerge our own flesh, will, shortcomings, and desires under God's bigger and better plan. God will not violate our will and give us what we don't want or ask for so in this stage, we learn to submit ourselves under God. We therefore have to partner with the Holy Spirit to reveal to us the true underlying issues that need to be addressed and then pray with specificity. Any-way-you-bless-me prayer requests rarely work because it's hard to recognize their manifestation when they appear and then attribute them back to God.

The more we align ourselves with the Holy Spirit and obey Him in prayer and in everyday activities, the more responses to our prayers we will see. I truly believe that especially in the supplication stage, we should make time to pray in the Holy Spirit (or in other tongues). We ask the Lord to reveal to us what He was praying for and through us. Paul tells us that he prays in the spirit and he prays with his mind, thereby effectively stopping his mind from wandering by engaging it. The more we practice this secret, the more will find that He will show us what to say when we pray out of our own understanding (1 Cor. 12:13-14). But we have to ask Him for interpretation or understanding. We will never know more than the Holy Spirit does. We know that He searches the mind of Christ and prays it for us when we speak in tongues. It's therefore in our best interest to consult Him, even on what and how to pray. Pray in the Holy Spirit frequently and seek to grow in the length of time you spend praying in the Holy Spirit. Ask Him for insight on what you just prayed and He will shed light on your path.

**Word:** Once we have properly aligned ourselves by understanding what is really at stake, we have to find the relevant Word of God that is the antidote to the issue confronting us. We aren't praying our complaints or feelings. Instead, we are praying God's mind about said complaint back to Himself and commanding everything contrary to align with His Word so His Kingdom can come to this earth even as it is in Heaven. Jesus very clearly stated that we could have whatever we wanted and prayed but only under these two conditions: abide in me and let my Words abide in you (John 15:7).

**Internalize**: To internalize and meditate refers to the real process by which we take the Word of God, chew on it, and assimilate it into our spirit man. In the Jewish tradition, meditating involves actively taking the scripture and literally rehearsing and muttering it under our breath, memorizing it into our minds:

> *Keep this Book of the Law always on your lips; meditate on it day and night*, so that you may be careful to do everything written in it. Then you will be prosperous and successful" (Joshua 1:8, NIV).

We then take that Word and meditate on it until faith arises and we are able to visualize it:

> Now faith is the substance of things hoped for, the evidence of things not seen. (Hebrews 11:1, KJV).

Once we reach that point of being able to see the intangible on the canvas of our spirits, we can then go forward to the next step.

**Declare:** To declare means to announce or claim openly and aloud. In this case, the applicable Word of God and names of God to your situation. My dear Royal Prayer Warrior, you have to announce to your present situation what the truth of God's Word says and by faith stand on that truth. You will have what you say for life and death are on your tongue. You should speak in whatever dominant language you communicate in when you are declaring the Word of God.

**Exercise Authority**: This is where we put on our armor and wield our weapons of warfare to contend for the things that are in principle ours, but could be challenged or besieged by the enemy. We exercise our authority by resisting and subduing any rogue situations that are not complying to the Word and Will of God. We also exercise our authority by declaring, casting down, trampling, destroying, the works of the enemy and prophetically speaking the Word of God into reality instead. Elements of Adoration and Declaration will come back into play even while in this area because Satan hates to hear the Word (and it is your sword) and hates to be reminded of the supremacy of Jesus. Praising Jesus, especially talking and singing about His blood and power weakens our enemy and facilitates our victory. While exercising authority and wrestling in prayer, pivot your focus back to Jesus, the author and finisher of your faith, and be generous in your praise of Him. The enemy should never have more focus or attention than Jesus.

**Repeat:** As you patiently wait to see your prayer answered, continue to give thanks, profess, and superimpose the desired result over your situation. Continue to practice the steps leading up to this point and periodically consult with the Holy Spirit if you are on the right path or if anything needs to be tweaked or changed.

**Manifestation:** This is where we get to possess in the natural that which we have been nurturing and contending for in the spirit. Obviously, manifestation will bring additional Adoration and Thanksgiving.

Now, here's an important note for clarity. Not every one of these steps are needed every single time we pray. Ultimately, to attain a healthy prevailing prayer life, all these elements of prayer must come into play to varying degrees and at different stages, certain components will take more precedence than at other times. Allow the Holy Spirit to guide you.

## Hindrances to a Lifestyle of Prevailing, Slaying, and Reigning

Because our enemy thrives in darkness, obscurity, and ignorance, we may have a mental understanding of the things that aren't in our best interest, yet not necessarily recognize them when they show up in our lives. Satan blinds the eyes of men, even Christians, so we don't discern or acknowledge when we are confronted by the things that hinder our growth to power and greatness. He doesn't want us to be all that we were designed to be. He will figure out all kinds of devices by which we can be limited or stopped. Therefore, it is always in our best interest when we don't understand our feelings and or circumstances to ask the Holy Spirit to help us process what is really at the root of it.

**Doubt:** When we doubt, we are uncertain about something we once were at least partially on board with. The less grounded we are in the revelation of what we believe in or are asking for, the easier it is for doubt to creep in. One of my favorite expressions is "A man with an experience is never at the mercy of another with a theory." If any of the foundational concepts I have shared over the course of this book remains only a theory to you, it will be easy for a contrary voice to take away the head knowledge (or theory) you have been introduced to. This is why it is important to have your own personal revelation and to spend time assimilating the Word and making the various verses shared your own. It will produce a firm foundation upon which even winds and waves from the storms of life will be unable to dislodge from you.

> Therefore, my dear brothers and sisters, stand firm. Let nothing move you. Always give yourselves fully to the work of the Lord, because you know that your labor in the Lord is not in vain. (1 Corinthians 15:58, NIV).

The opposite of doubt is steadfastness the state of not being easily shaken. 1 Corinthians 15:58 instructs us to stand firm and let nothing move us. We have to be convinced that God is who His Word says He is, that His promises are for sure and for real. We must be convinced that our labors are not in vain and God will come through for us. Like the widow in the Parable of the Unjust Judge (Luke 18:1-8) who didn't stop believing her case would be vindicated, we have to keep at it and believe we will see our desired results.

The simplest way to deal with doubt is to drown it out with more Word of God, past examples of successes, whether ours or others. (This is why gratitude is so important! It reminds us of what God has done!) We overcome by our testimony. This is why seeing the raw evidence of God's power at work in healings, miracles, signs, and the gifts of the Spirit, are helpful to our own ability to cleave to the Lord and be steadfast. We should also take our doubts to the Lord and ask for Him to send us whatever is necessary to firm our grip on Him.

**Double-Mindedness**: Double-mindedness refers to a swinging from one point of view to another, or wavering like a leaf being blown in the wind. It tends to come from a deep place of instability than uncertainty. The Word commands us to resist the devil, immediately followed by an admonition to draw near to God by cleansing our hands from sin and purifying our hearts from double-mindedness (James 4:7-8). When we are double-minded, our hearts are not pure because we have divided interests. In a sense, we are practicing spiritual adultery and so we erode our own prayers and hinder our answers from materializing. The Bible states clearly that if we are double-minded we shouldn't expect God to answer us (James 1:5-6). To deal with it requires an earnest acknowledgement of the issue and deliberately seeking the power of God to address and heal the underlying issues causing our lack of loyalty to God.

**Fear:** Fear can come in all forms. It can be crippling and sudden. More frequently fear is an instinctual or primal feeling that can lie hovering and unrecognized in the background of our minds and spirits. Fear puts the brakes on obedience, faith, and our love for God and His ways. Fear limits, controls, muzzles, and cheats us out of our full potential and the enemy then takes advantage of our compromise to fear by bludgeoning us over the head with the same inadequacies. Ultimately, fear left unchecked afflicts or torments. The Bible says perfect love casts out fear and that at the judgment seat, we will have boldness (the opposite of fear) because as He is, so are we (1 John 4:17-18).

I encourage you, dear reader, that if you heard from the Lord on a particular instruction, do it, and if necessary, do it afraid. Do it, even while reminding Him of His promises to you. Jacob modeled the Royal Prayer Warrior (Genesis 32:6-11) when he was finally going back to the Land God had promised him, even though it meant confronting his brother Esau first. He was sorely distressed (verse 7) because he knew that Jacob and his family were severely outnumbered by his approaching brother. Esau was flanked by four hundred armed men. So Jacob prayed, first reminding God that it was His instruction he was following (verse 9), humbly showed gratitude for the things he had already been blessed to experience (verse 10) and then pleaded for deliverance from the hand of his brother (verse 11). He then followed up his prayer with yet another reminder of God's Word to God.

When we sense a reluctance to throw ourselves heartily into some directive the Lord has given us, ask Him to help us examine our hearts to see if there is any fear lurking in there. We then have to come against the source of that fear and ask for boldness and confidence in the power of the Lord to walk without fear.

**Lack of accompanying actions:** Faith without works is dead (James 2:26). At some point in matters big and small, we will be required to prove our love for the Father, just as Abraham was asked to sacrifice Isaac. God can't be mocked and He knows everything about us. God doesn't want us to be people who only serve Him with our lips, but also who serve Him with hearts and consequently, in our actions (Isaiah 29:13). In fact, He considers such inaction a mockery. We have to be careful to be doers and not just hearers, to not just pray but also follow up with actions. We have to consult with the Holy Spirit in each situation exactly what those accompanying actions should be because it isn't always evident.

**Anxiety:** Anxiety isn't always crippling and absolute even though it can be characterized as such as well. It can be quite subtle, yet still have a powerfully negating effect on our ability to pray and or see manifestation. Anxiety can be a generalized, nebulous feeling of unease which can be hard to pinpoint yet subtly lurks just beneath the surface of our hearts. At the root of all anxiety is an expectation (sometimes inexplicable) of things going wrong and can include tension, feelings of dread or impending doom. Anxiety is the opposite of peace and the path to overcoming anxiety is found below:

> Do not be anxious about anything, but in every situation, by prayer and petition, with thanksgiving, present

your requests to God. ⁷ And the peace of God, which transcends all understanding, will guard your hearts and your minds in Christ Jesus. (Philippians. 4:6-7, NIV).

**Disobedience**: Any of the other hindrances to prevailing prayer boil down to disobedience. It can be deliberate or unintentional but the end result is still the same: disobedience can slow or even completely cancel out the manifestation of our prayers and the promises of God.

**Anger and Unforgiveness**: The Bible tells us that Moses was a powerful prophet and man of prayer. He was a very meek man but he did get angry on occasion. Unfortunately, that anger denied Him the ability to set foot in the Promised Land. Anger can keep us away from enjoying all the manifestations of our prayers. Jesus shows us this is very important to the manifestation of our prayers. He commands us to stop praying to the Father and first deal with any offense we may have caused a brother or sister before coming back into the presence of the Lord (Mark 11:25-26). Similarly, Paul instructs the Corinthian church to forgive a brother so Satan can't outwit or have an advantage over them (2 Cor. 2:5-11). It would be a shame to put in all this work only for the enemy to circumvent our blessings because we chose to remain in unforgiveness.

**Ignorance**: A lack of knowledge of the things of God is a great setback because knowledge is power. It is therefore critical to keep asking the Holy Spirit to lead and guide you where He wants you to be, and to send you whatever is lacking in your faith at the specific time. This is necessary because it's needed to get you to your next level. Ask for help. Ask for direction and re-direction frequently. If you are hungry and demonstrate your hunger to Him, He will come through for you. If you insist on being close-minded and satisfied with what you already have and think you know, He will not be obligated to keep pushing you where you refuse to go. Remember, He is the Good Shepherd and you are the sheep. Sheep aren't exactly known for their street smarts or brightness. There's a difference between not knowing, and knowing and not doing better. It's ok to acknowledge to Him that your knowledge is limited and you need His wisdom, guidance, and direction.

**Indiscipline**: the practicalities of prevailing prayer won't serve you very long if you don't practice prayer. The practice, or habit, of prayer is what allows you to build spiritual muscles and stamina or endurance, just as the practice of regularly going to the gym and lifting weights will ultimately culminate in a stronger body. The habit of praying regularly is initially hard work but as you continue, it gets easier to access the presence of God. Even the process of figuring out what to say to Him becomes easier. The conversation on your end flows smoothly and you hear from God faster. You are able to sense His leading, and there is less confusion.

**Impatience**: Many believers strike out in their prayer lives due to impatience (you charge me as guilty here). Undoubtedly, we want everything immediately, if not yesterday. But our timing isn't always God's timing. He is more interested in the process of us being conformed to the image of His dear son Jesus, than our instant gratification or comfort. It is through faith and patience that we inherit the promises of God. Jesus, in the Parable of the Sower (Luke 8:15) explains that the ones who fall in good soil and bear forth much fruit do so with patience.

**A lack of engagement**: Your soul has to be anchored in consistent engagement. You don't want your prayer rolling off your lips while your heart is far away. You are simply wasting your time if all you are doing is fulfilling one more thing on your daily checklist to ease your conscience. Remember, God rewards those who *diligently* seek Him (Hebrews 11:6), not half-heartedly or disinterestedly. It is helpful to visualize yourself having an audience with your Heavenly Father or the King of Kings or the Great Judge or whatever characteristic of God you chose. If you were meeting the Queen of England or the President of the United States, you would certainly be excited and engaged. You would be even more so if you knew that meeting was your only hope to getting or accomplishing something you would otherwise never see materialize, like a presidential pardon. If you think you have other options available outside of Christ, if God isn't made your source and foremost desire, a lifestyle of connected prayer will always be optional for you. Becoming mentally and spiritually connected has to be a priority for any serious believer. It is self-sufficiency which is a form of pride that keeps us disconnected from God. If we believe we can handle or tolerate whatever our circumstances are by ourselves, there will be no need for us to rely on Him. Engaged prayer will be optional.

**Negative Confession**: Speaking things that are contrary to the promises of God that we have been professing can abort the manifestation of the fullness of our prayers. Most Christians don't realize this but in the spirit realm, our enemies speak negative things over us all time, in an attempt to pass their wicked agendas into our lives. If we line up with them by speaking negatively, we possibly could delay or deny ourselves our blessings.

Even our seemingly harmless and idle words can have negative implications. We must watch our words and they must be carefully weighed to make sure they aren't running contrary to God. Things like "I never catch a good break" or "I'm never going to be happy." Words that express doubt and unbelief can be detrimental to our success in prayer. Even though Zechariah was a priest and served God faithfully, his disposition wasn't right. God had to shut his mouth until John the Baptist was born and given his name because Zechariah ran the risk of messing things up with his mouth. Our positive confessions and declarations must drown out the negative words of the enemy who doesn't wish to see our destiny come through.

## The Proper Mindset for the Prevailing Prayer Warrior

### Focus, Fervency, and Intensity

I have a confession to make. I wasn't always a woman of focus or discipline. I will admit that even now, I don't always have an easy time of staying on target in prayer. As mentioned before, I naturally have a very hyperactive mind that daydreamed and wondered all over all over while I was in school. It has taken a lot of prayer (yes, I know - prayer about prayer!), mindfulness and the power of the Holy Spirit to bring my mind under some measure of control to have victory in this area for prevailing prayer. I had to cry out to the Lord, battle myself and my thoughts to see the needle begin to move in my favor. And to be honest, this is who I am and so I have come to realize that it's part of my flesh that needs to continually be crucified. My level of engagement and interest had to ratchet up significantly to see results come through. Focusing takes place not only during the actual prayer itself, but also before and after because we are to watch and pray. Successful prayer requires much strategizing and intense watchfulness.

This is why I emphasize the mindset coaching aspect of my ministry because our battle begins in the mind; our battlefield is in our minds and unfortunately many Christians barely leave out the gate for their battles because they are not adequately geared up mentally for the fight (1 Peter 1:13).

In addition to focusing, I have also come to realize I am much more successful in prayer when I harness my energies and channel or concentrate my emotions when praying. We have all heard about how people perform acts of strength under extreme duress. For example, a car rolls over and pins a small child. The desperate parent suddenly gains supernatural strength long enough to budge the car to rescue the kid. It's the same concept in prayer. We first need a certain all-consuming intensity or zeal and a deep-seated desire to change that situation. We then have to harness and apply that emotion to prayer in order to see some supernatural movement in our favor.

When Jesus told us to "ask, seek and knock" (Matt. 7:7-8, Luke 11:9-10). He was referring to different types of prayer. The translated root word from which we get the word "ask" actually refers to an intense, deep-seated desire. If we are going to be Royal Prayer Warriors we have to be filled with burning desire and intensity to get our petitions fulfilled. We have to be fired up for the faith fight; we can't be casual or disengaged about how we approach God to make our requests known. We can't be disinterested or disaffected when we are fighting the enemy and pushing back the gates of Hell by binding, casting and loosing. Who would we be kidding? We can't go through the motions simply to convince ourselves that we have done what was requested of us. God is neither impressed nor obligated to answer under such circumstances and neither will our enemy be moved by our cold and feeble attempts at resisting him because we didn't give him and his demons any real resistance in prayer. Similarly, when we are confessing the Word of God and super-imposing them over our natural circumstances, we have to say those verses like we mean them and that they really mean something to us.

If Jesus, who already knew He was God, still prayed fervent and engaged prayers, we are not exempt from having to do so. He could have commanded angels to come to His aid at any time and could have taken all kinds of shortcuts yet, He modeled the Royal Prayer Warrior approach to prayer that is required of us all:

> During the days of Jesus' life on Earth, he offered up prayers and petitions with fervent cries and tears to the one who could save him from death, *and he was heard* because of his reverent submission. (Hebrews 5:7, NIV).

Many people are put off by outward displays of emotion and reject real biblical prayer, saying things like "it doesn't take all, God already knows what is in my heart." True prayer *does* take all of that and then some. Refuse to allow yourself to give a stiff upper-lipped devotion to God; it isn't the model the Author and Finisher of our Faith ascribed to and it certainly doesn't move the hand of God again and again.

## SUBMISSION AND CHILD-LIKE FAITH

Submitting to God affords us the ability to resist the Devil. But we can't effectively carry out spiritual warfare if we aren't giving our Captain the obedience and honor that is rightfully His: we can't be rogue agents doing our own thing. To submit means to yield, in the same way in traffic, when there is a yield sign, we are required to let the other driver have right of way. God wants right of way in our lives. God wants us to submerge our own desires and will under His, just as Jesus did. Jesus submitted to God's painful plan of the cross and this is how He ultimately was able to resist and beat the Devil at his own game. We are still enjoying the fruits of His spoils, two thousand years later and His blood still conquers the enemy. If we don't submit, the enemy will not flee from us. Our victories will be compromised at best, or even non-existent.

Child-like faith is a certain simplicity of heart that allows us to unquestioningly and quickly obey God, especially as we are impressed upon to do so. Child-like faith is born out of relationship and comes from an instinctual place of trust in the Lord, in His goodness and fatherly nature. Child-like faith Jesus made it clear that entering the Kingdom without child-like faith is simply not possible (Mark 10:15). Child-like faith isn't looking for ways in which our Father could let us down or be untrue. Neither is it driven by the need to rationalize, understand, and explain everything before we do it. Child-like faith requires a humbling of oneself, a pulling down of mental strongholds, and a conscious conversion or repentance in one's mind to align our thinking to God's thinking:

> And said, "Verily I say unto you, Except ye be converted, and become as little children, ye shall not enter into the kingdom of heaven. Whosoever therefore shall humble himself as this little child, the same is greatest in the kingdom of heaven." (Matthew 18:3-4, KJV).

Child-like faith is acquired as we humble and submit our mind and thought processes to the mind of Christ. God's ways and thoughts are not like ours (Isaiah 55:6-9), hence the need for us to forsake our ways (attitudes, process of seeing, understanding, and thinking) for His. If we want to experience power and greatness in the Kingdom of God, Child-like faith is essential.

## A Warrior's Heart: Pit Bull Tenacity, Stamina, and a Willingness to Wrestle and Work

There is a level of praying where prayer is likened to wrestling (Col. 4:12 and Eph. 6:12). In Genesis 32, Jacob was returning home after years of hiding at his uncle's and an inevitable meeting with the brother he had cheated loomed ominously before him. He was rightfully worried and desperate for God to intervene. Jacob prayed for deliverance from his twin brother and safe passage.

Later that night, Jacob was drawn into that higher dimension of wresting prayer when he was accosted by a man who tussled with him till daybreak. Somehow, Jacob recognized that the fight he was in was tied to the manifestation of the prophecy that he was going to be the greater of the twins and he had to wrestle hard and long to settle the matter once and for all. Like a pit bull, he locked his jaws hung on and fought for dear life! Eventually, the man was forced to bless Jacob in order to be released from his grip. (Genesis 32:24-30). Jacob's tenacity, stamina, and willingness to get down and dirty got him his manifestation. He was completely changed and given a new name, Israel, as a result. Israel means a Prince who has power with God and man and has prevailed! I believe this is the name we are all called to have as true Believers. We are Prevailing Prayer Warriors!

Prevailing prayer is work (Rom. 15:30) and requires labor, exertion, and striving. It requires both quantity and quality time in the presence of the Lord. Jesus often prayed all night or woke up early before dawn to pray (Luke 6:12, Mark 1:35). He was able to accomplish much in his three-year ministry not because He was the Son of God, but because He was a praying human. No transportation to enter Jerusalem? He prayed and then by revelation, knew where to find a donkey to fulfill His need. When Jesus needed money for taxes, His prevailing prayer life provided the much-needed guidance on where to find the money: in the mouth of a fish, no less. Only two fish and five loaves for at least five thousand people? No problem there. He just prayed and before they knew it, there were overflowing baskets of left-overs.

I don't believe Jesus started this practice of prevailing prayer only when He officially went into ministry. In fact, it is almost impossible to just start by jumping into a forty-day fast without some prior practice. Jesus the Son of Man had to build the stamina for prayer and fasting over time. Building our stamina in prayer, developing a warrior's heart and persevering to the end are well worth the journey. The ensuing trade-off includes acquiring spiritual power, freedom, rewards, and the blessings of a vibrant relationship with God.

Dear Reader, may God grant you a warrior's heart to stay the course of prevailing prayer so you can truly enjoy the proof of having been with God.

## THE PROOF OF PREVAILING PRAYER

Finally, let's look at the spoils that come from living a life of prevailing prayer. We know that God rewards those who diligently seek Him and we can rest assured that as we have made time for Him, and drawn closer to Him in prayer, He will not allow us to remain empty-handed. What then are some of the evidence of prevailing prayer at work in our lives?

The following are but a few:

## HALLMARKS OF A ROYAL PREVAILING PRAYER WARRIOR

Now that we have discussed the practice of prevailing prayer, it will be up to you to desire to go from pitiful to powerful so you can enjoy the benefits that come with being a Royal Prayer Warrior. Here are but a few of the advantages that come with deliberately applying yourself to the guidelines set forth in this book, with the help of the Holy Spirit. As you work through these steps of acquiring and applying the Word of God, and using them in your prayer life, you will start to notice maturity and personal growth in areas you may not even have known you were lacking to begin with. Additionally, your continued obedience in practicing these principles will only further enlarge your spirit man's power and capacity to pray, slay and reign. Here are some of the attributes you can expect to see in your overall

Christian walk as you build the habit of regularly implementing the steps delineated here:

## Greater levels of the fruit and quality of gift(s) of the Spirit (Galatians 5:22).

If you make it a point to pray in the Holy Spirit more frequently and for longer durations, you will find that peace, joy, love, patience, and all the other fruit will manifest and be more available in your life. Especially if you are connected to an assembly of Believers, at least one spiritual gift will start to emerge as you seek earnestly for it. It will then be your responsibility to train yourself to use the gift and grow in the strength of that gift. Remember that spiritual gifts are for edifying the Body of Christ, not just so you can mark it off as another accomplishment for your personal entertainment. Your destiny will become clearer.

## More clarity in hearing from God, greater discernment in general and increased divine intervention in your life (Romans 8:14).

You will be pleasantly surprised to find your spiritual hearing to be more fine-tuned. You will realize that the Word of God will come alive in a new way to you. Verses will go from simple words on the pages to specific, tailored God-breathed communication with you and you will have direct assurance of the Lord leading you because there will frequently be confirmation from some other source, like a sermon at church or a phone call from somebody without prior knowledge re-affirming what you initially heard.

You will also experience other avenues by which He will communicate with you. For example, prior to committing to the prevailing prayer lifestyle, I slept like a log and almost never remembered any dreams. As I asked the Lord to reveal His secrets to me for my life and to show me my destiny, my dream life started changing. Even though I'm out like a light bulb almost as soon as I get into bed, the important things God wants me to know often come in dreams that linger in my psyche after I awake. I don't always comprehend the dreams but I have learned to always pray and ask the

Holy Spirit to give me understanding and the right approach to counter-act whatever the dream meant. The Lord has used dreams to warn me about attacks to come, and then subsequently, He has given me strategies on what to pray for concerning others and myself, and many more. John 16:13 tells us that the Holy Spirit guides us into all truth; He tells us what He hears and shows us things to come. This is another reason praying in the Holy Spirit and asking the Lord for understanding is so important. I have become a better wife and mother as a result of this.

On the discernment front, it will be easier to recognize when things aren't in alignment with the Word and Will of God for you specifically. In short, God will give you insight, revelation and fore-warning from the Holy Spirit who shows us things to come and the secrets needed for successful warfare.

The bottom line is the Lord wants us to have more control and power in our lives. We are not to be upstaged all the time by unanticipated problems that we could have pre-emptively and proactively dealt with in prayer.

## Increasing reliance on the Holy Spirit

As you experience the first two points, you will find yourself even more in need of the Holy Spirit because your ability to tap into His power gives you such leverage that you feel vulnerable without regular appointments with Him. You realize how frail we really are and how deeply we need God to truly function as the peculiar people and royal kings and priests He designed us to be. Your increased reliance on the Holy Spirit will allow you to be spirit-led as opposed to flesh-led thereby elevating us to walk in the true Son-ship status He has assigned for us (Romans 8:14.) Additionally, because the Holy Spirit prays for us and helps us in our weaknesses (Romans 8:26-27) we are given a leg up on the rest of the world, a secret source of insight and power that we simply can't do without.

## GREATER FREQUENCY OF ANSWERED PRAYER AND OCCURRENCE OF MIRACLES, COUPLED WITH A DEEPER LEVEL AND LIFESTYLE OF PRAYER:

Increasing reliance on the Holy Spirit takes us to a deeper level and lifestyle of prayer, which in turn brings more answered prayer. These two benefits go hand in hand and tend to feed off of one another. Miracles, breakthroughs and answered prayers will become the norm in your life. God is just as interested in the accomplishment of our most mundane activities as He is in the big things for His Kingdom. He is just as delighted to listen to and answer both types of prayer. In fact, the smaller answered prayers tend to reinforce our faith levels and make us bolder to ask for even bigger things. I am at a point in my life where I ask God about all kinds of things and He answers without fail. Some answers come very quickly, others may take a while so I keep hammering on them. But I am confident that I have my desired results. Not even the long-awaited, seemingly elusive ones shake my faith in Him because I know He is working on everything together for my good.

## STRONGER ANOINTING AND POWER ON YOUR LIFE

By using the authority Jesus gave us when He breathed the Holy Spirit upon us, we will see the anointing and power in our lives become stronger. One of the most influential things I ever read was by Kenneth E. Hagin in the legacy edition of his book "The Believer's Authority." In a segment on how to deal with demons, he writes:

> "You can exercise spiritual authority over others as long as they are in your presence. You can take authority over all unseen forces. If you learn how to exercise authority like this, it will work in your home as well. I've heard of women who exercised their spiritual authority when their unsaved husbands came home arguing and fighting. The women had learned how to quietly and calmly rebuke the evil spirits behind the situation and claim authority over them- and the situation changed."
> (Kenneth E. Hagin "The Believer's Authority." Page 81)

Hagin goes on to explain that exercising authority in this way isn't exercising authority over the individual's will, but over the spirit behind the behavior. I have learned how to sidestep so many family arguments, work misunderstandings, marital distress by implementing this secret of exercising my spiritual authority and not allowing the enemy to just play foul in my circumstances. I can't tell you how many disasters I have avoided this way.

### YOU WILL HAVE WHAT YOU SAY.

Your words both, good and evil, will become self-fulfilling prophecies. Job 22:27-28 says you will decree a thing and it will be established. Consequently, you will have to become very choosy with what comes out of your mouth because they carry the potential to create or destroy. Like Jesus who told the fig tree it would never bear fruit, a closer walk with the Lord will empower your words to align with your master's Words.

## TIPS AND THOUGHTS

1. Both quality and quantity of time spent before the Lord are important components of prevailing prayer. The goal is obviously to incrementally improve in both areas. What realistic goals are you willing to set for the actual practice section?
2. Which of the hindrances are you most likely to be a victim of and how do you plan to work with the Holy Spirit to prevail over them?
3. Based on the mindset section, which areas do you think come more naturally? Which ones will you need the most divine assistance?

## PRAYER POINTS

❖ Father, thank you for everything I have learned thus far. I pray in the mighty name of Jesus that you convert me from a mere hearer to a powerful doer. Amen.
❖ Great Jehovah, empower me to work on the mindsets and hindrances to being a royal prayer warrior.

- ❖ Holy Spirit, let the knowledge I have acquired move from my soul to my spirit. Give me grace to implement these principles with faith and patience.
- ❖ Lord, let me see evidence of your power in my life.
- ❖ Keep me connected to you Holy Spirit. I choose to rely on you and not on my own understanding. Increase my reliance on you.
- ❖ Let my life be filled with signs, wonders and breakthroughs to the praise and glory of your name.
- ❖ Let my prayer altar be set ablaze with your holy fire, Lord. Amen!

# PROLOGUE

In conclusion, thank you Dear Friend for coming with me on this introduction to a powerful and victorious overall Christian life, fueled by a lifestyle of prevailing prayer. If nothing else, I am sure that as you implement the foundational principles set forth in this book while utilizing the recommended mindset strategies, you will gain heightened confidence based on the God you know and according to His power that works in you.

Remember how confident David was when he came across Goliath? Prior to confronting Goliath, he had had practice overcoming life-threatening situations when he had killed a bear and a lion (1 Sam. 17:33-37). David knew his God intimately because he had developed a solid prayer and praise lifestyle; he spent countless hours writing and singing songs of worship and playing instruments before His Lord. His older brothers thought he was cocky, but he knew His God and was sure of the power that was at work in him. Everything God accomplishes through is us according to His power that is at work in us because He has no hands or feet here on Earth other than ours. No wonder Paul prays that we might be filled with all the fullness of God so that "He can do exceeding abundantly above all that we ask or think according to the power that works in us." (Eph. 3:19b-20).

The Bible tells us that after Jesus sent the disciples on a missions trip, they came back excited saying, "Lord, even devils obey us." (Luke 10:1 KJV). They couldn't believe what power they possessed and the things they discovered they could do in Jesus' name! My Friend, I am confident this will be your story too: you will be amazed at the magnificence of the hope of glory within you, if you will let Christ fill you up like He is truly supposed to even as you pray, slay and reign.

The Holy Spirit will restore you so you can truly walk in your destiny and be all that God created you to be. To help you be accountable and keep you growing in the prevailing prayer lifestyle, our website www.prayslayandreign.com has several resources to complement this book. In fact, as previously stated, this book is really only just an introduction. Now the real work begins using the Prevailing Prayer Workbook Journal as well as a host of additional training resources. It's time for the real work to begin. Let's get to work on doing what we have learned for we want to hear "well done, thou good and faithful servant" from the Lord.

I look forward to coaching and cheering you on into this magnificent dimension of Christian discipleship and sharing additional hacks for today's busy Christian. I know you will get to the place where you rule and reign with Christ and partner with Him to accomplish great things on this earth realm for the Kingdom of God. Shalom!

Your Prayer Cheerleader,
Rosetta Bernasko